Positive Affirmations Coloring Book for Boys

by

Chloe Nallis

Published by Renuti®

Test Color Page

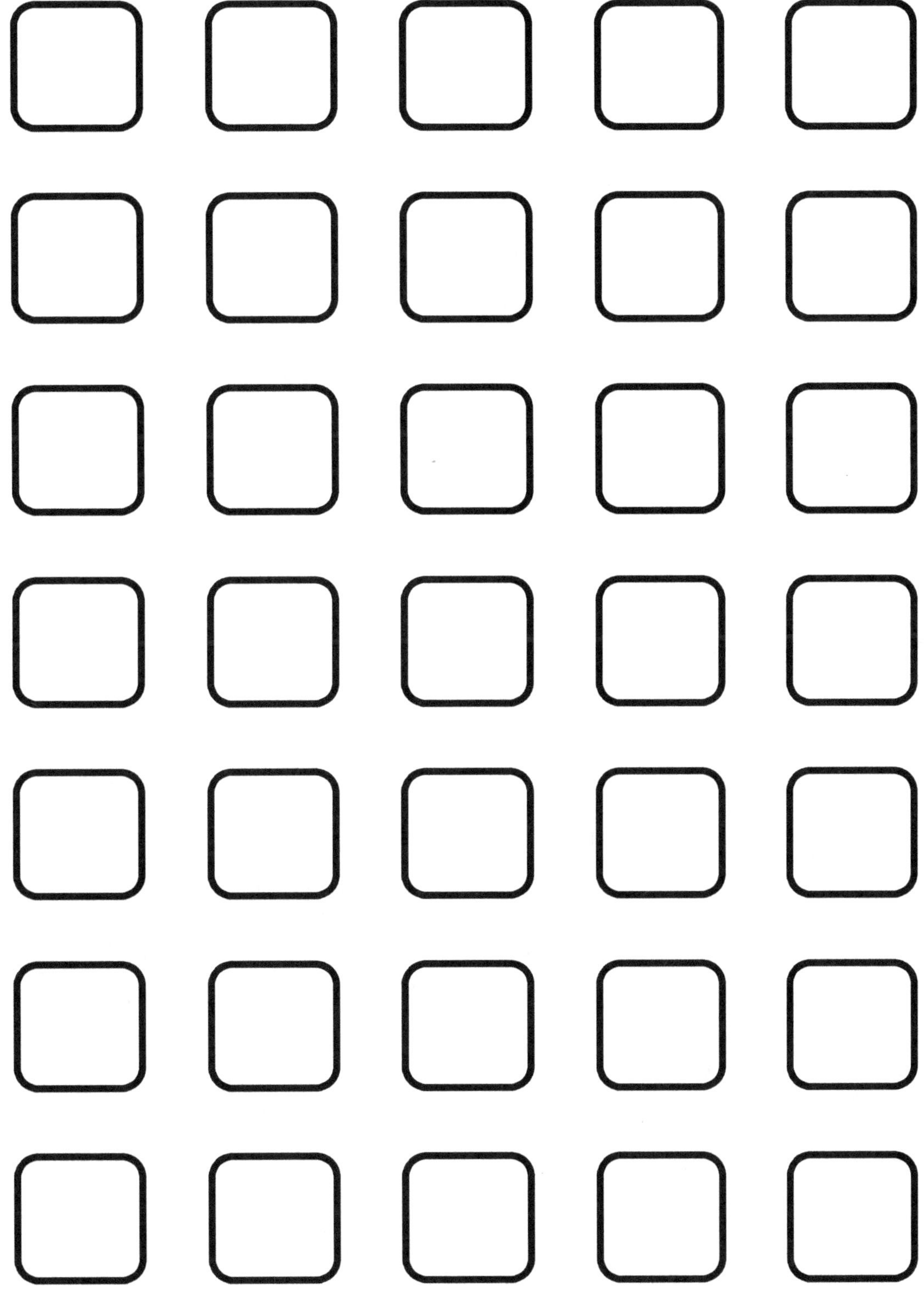

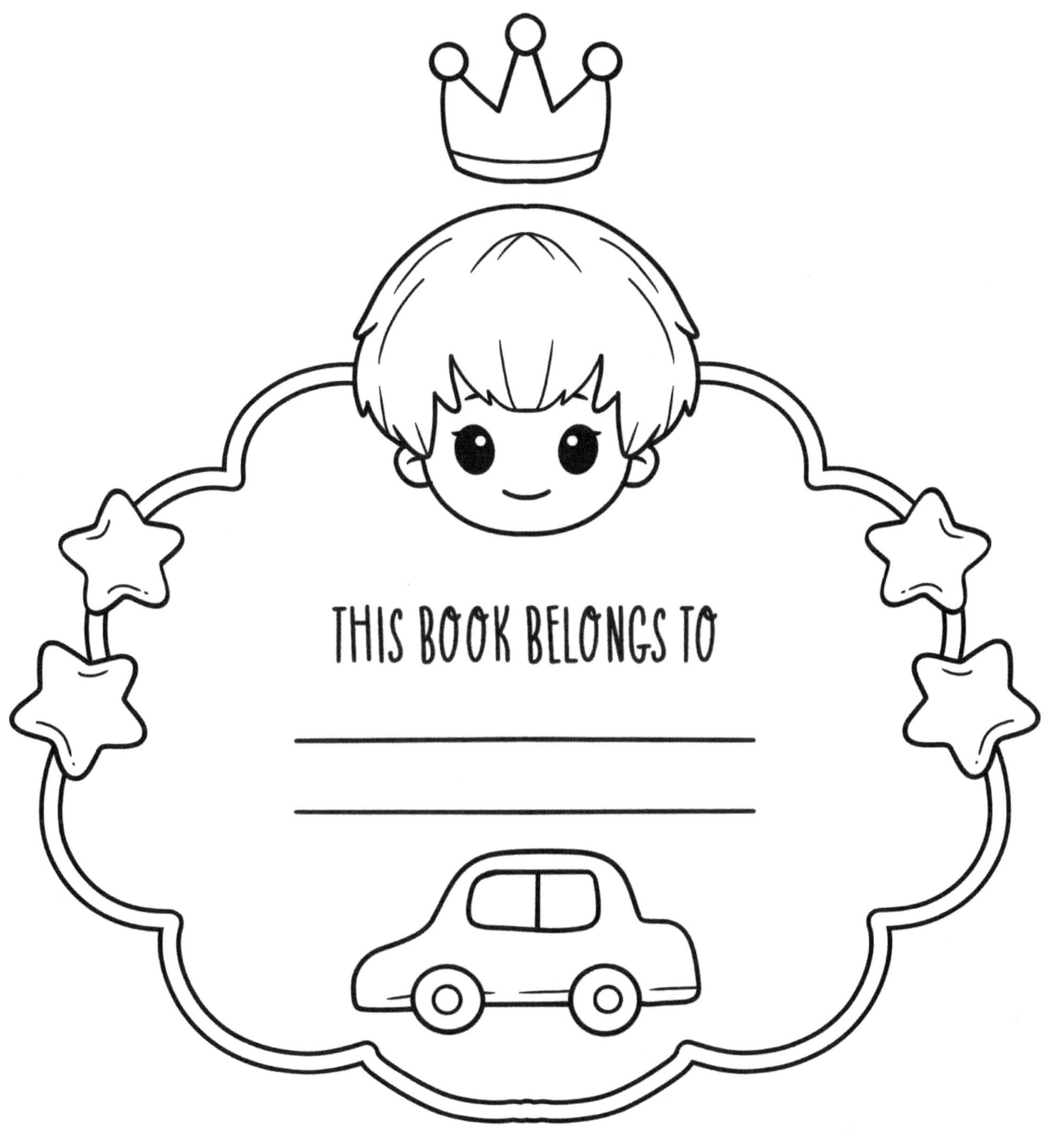
THIS BOOK BELONGS TO

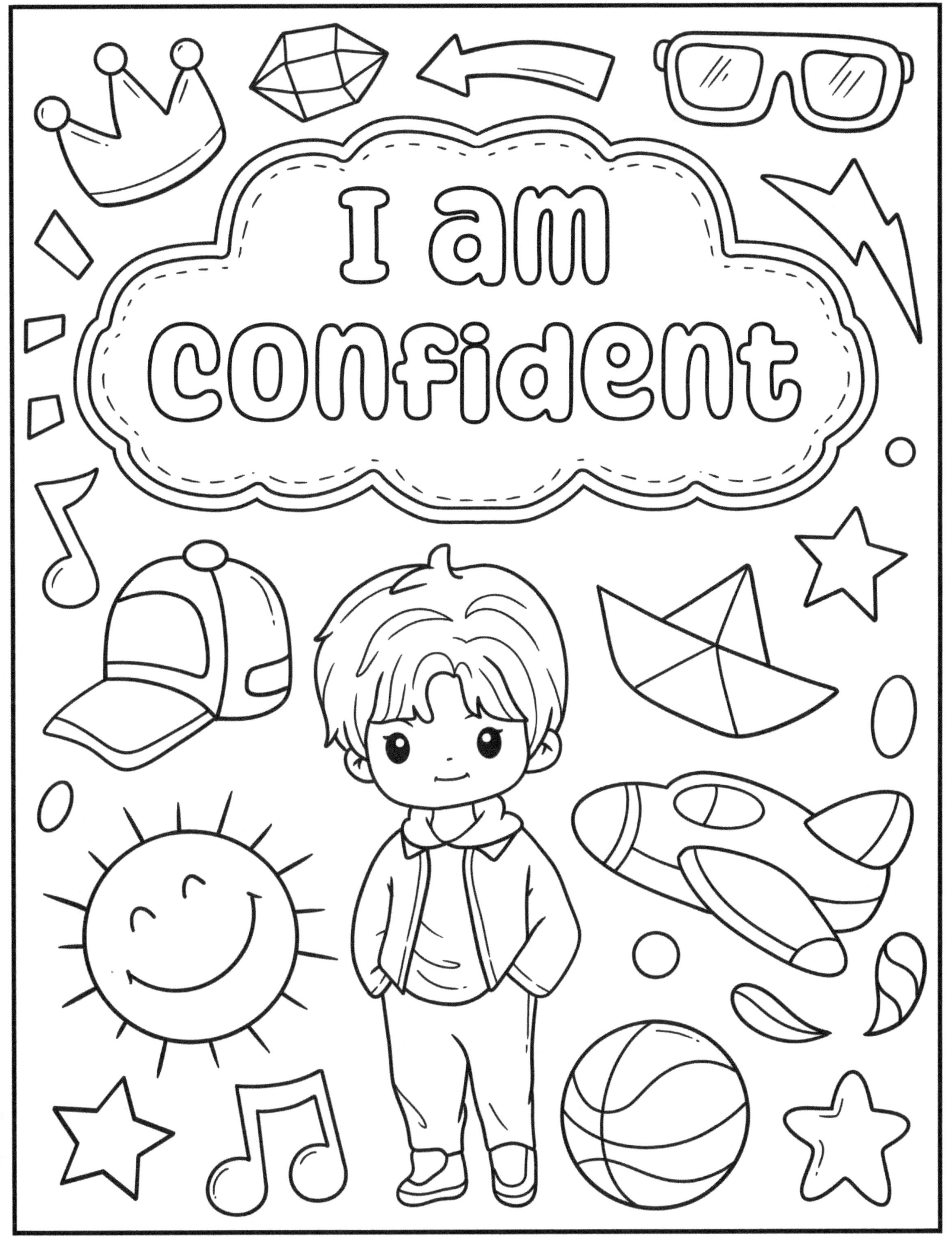
I am
confident

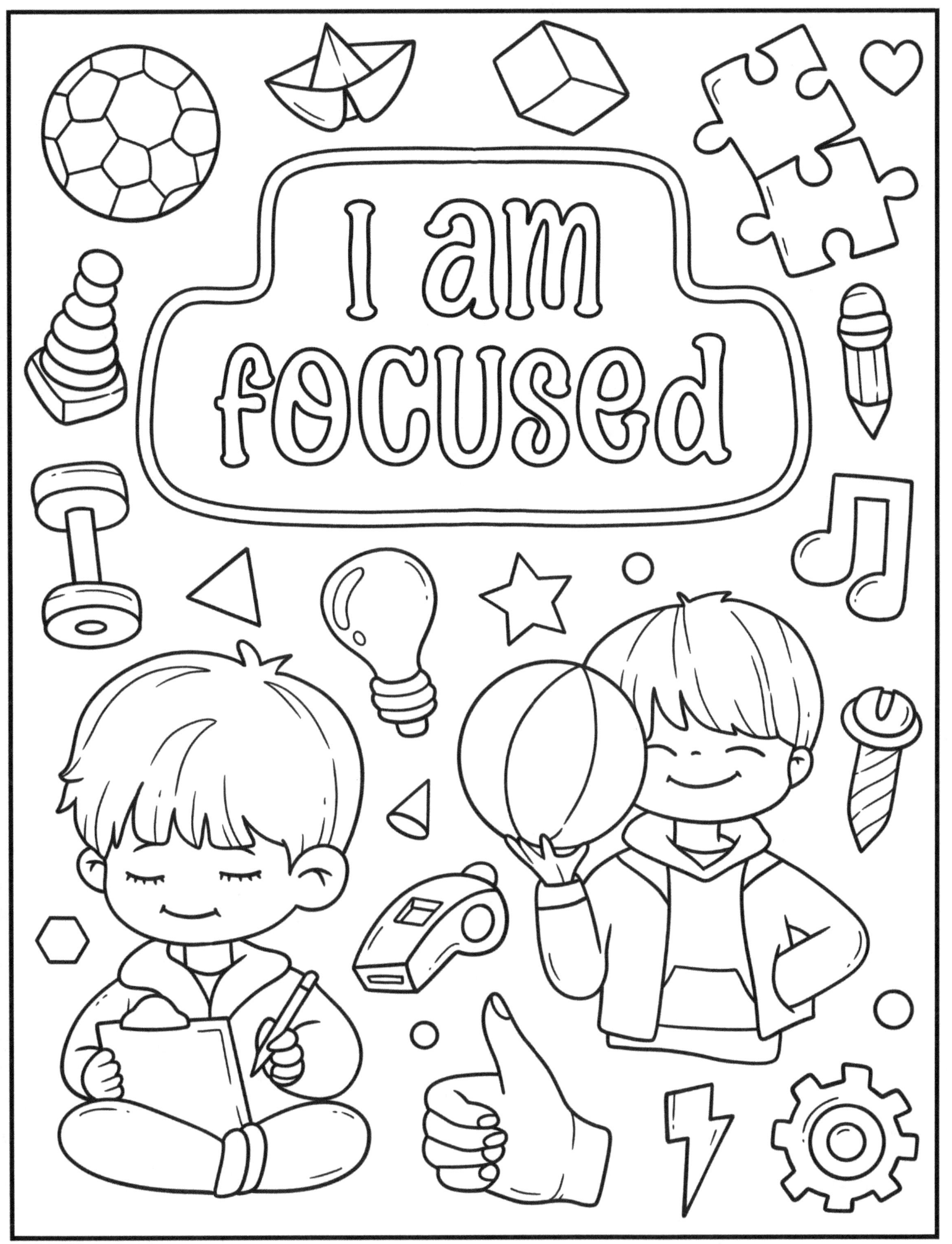
I am focused

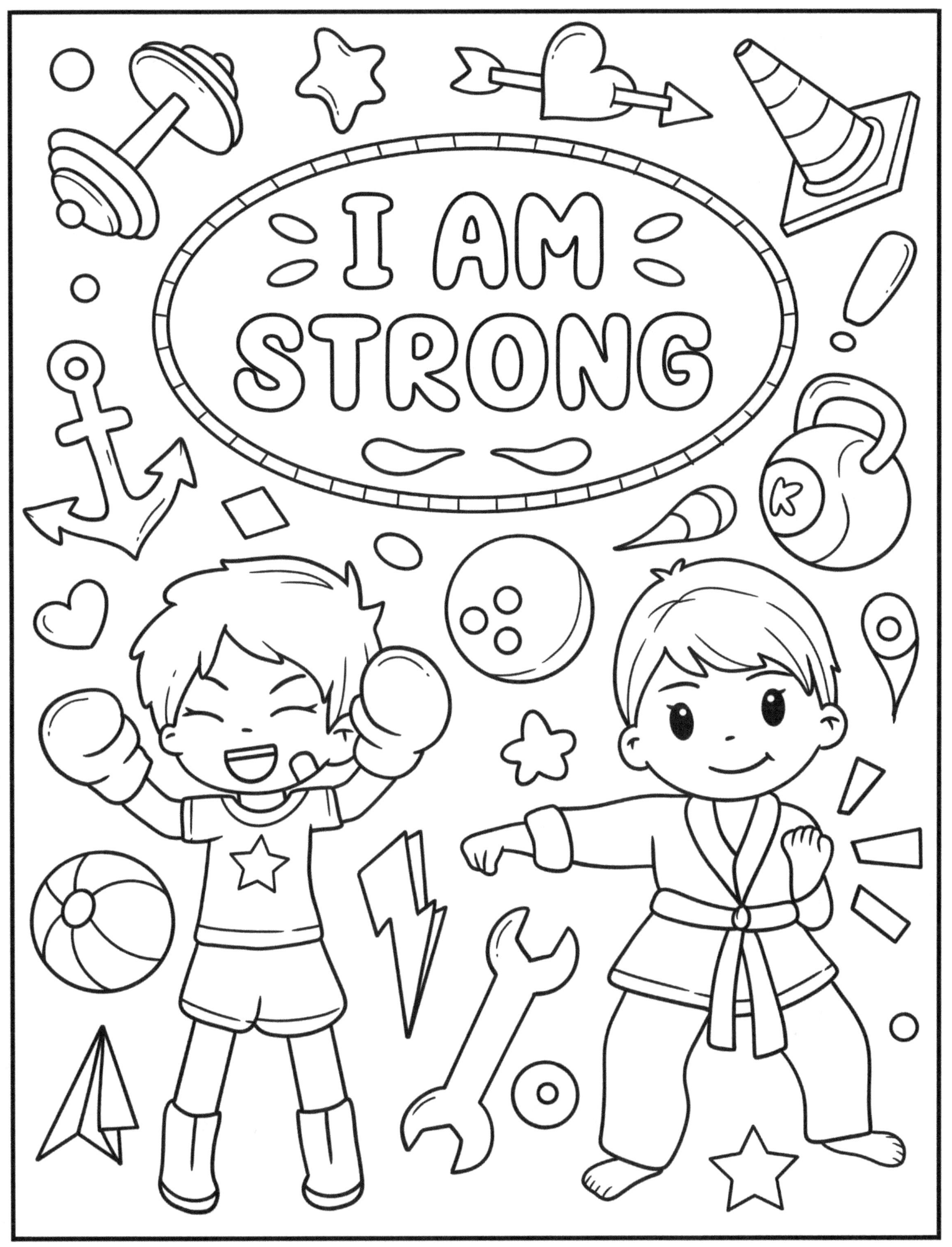
I AM
STRONG

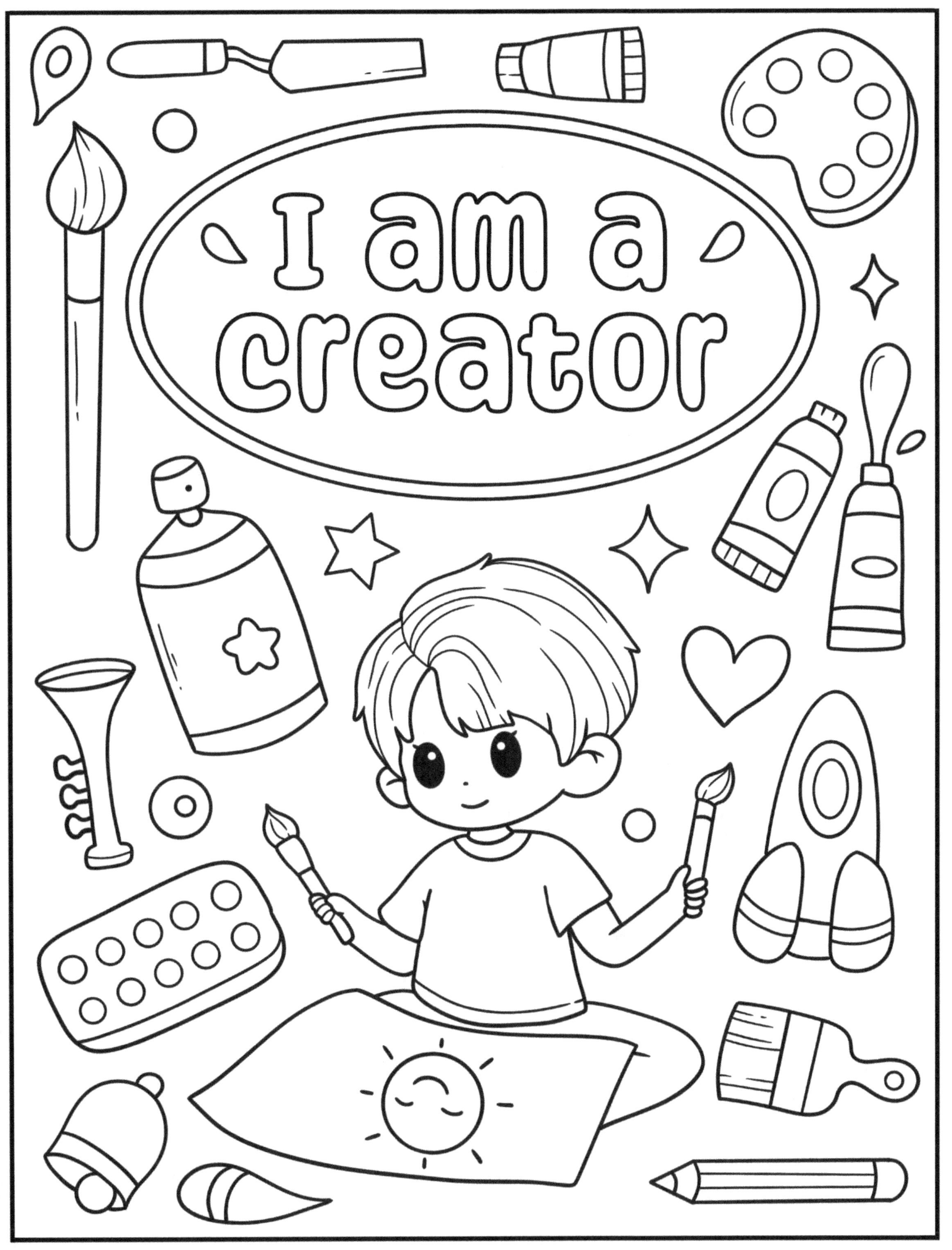
I am a
creator

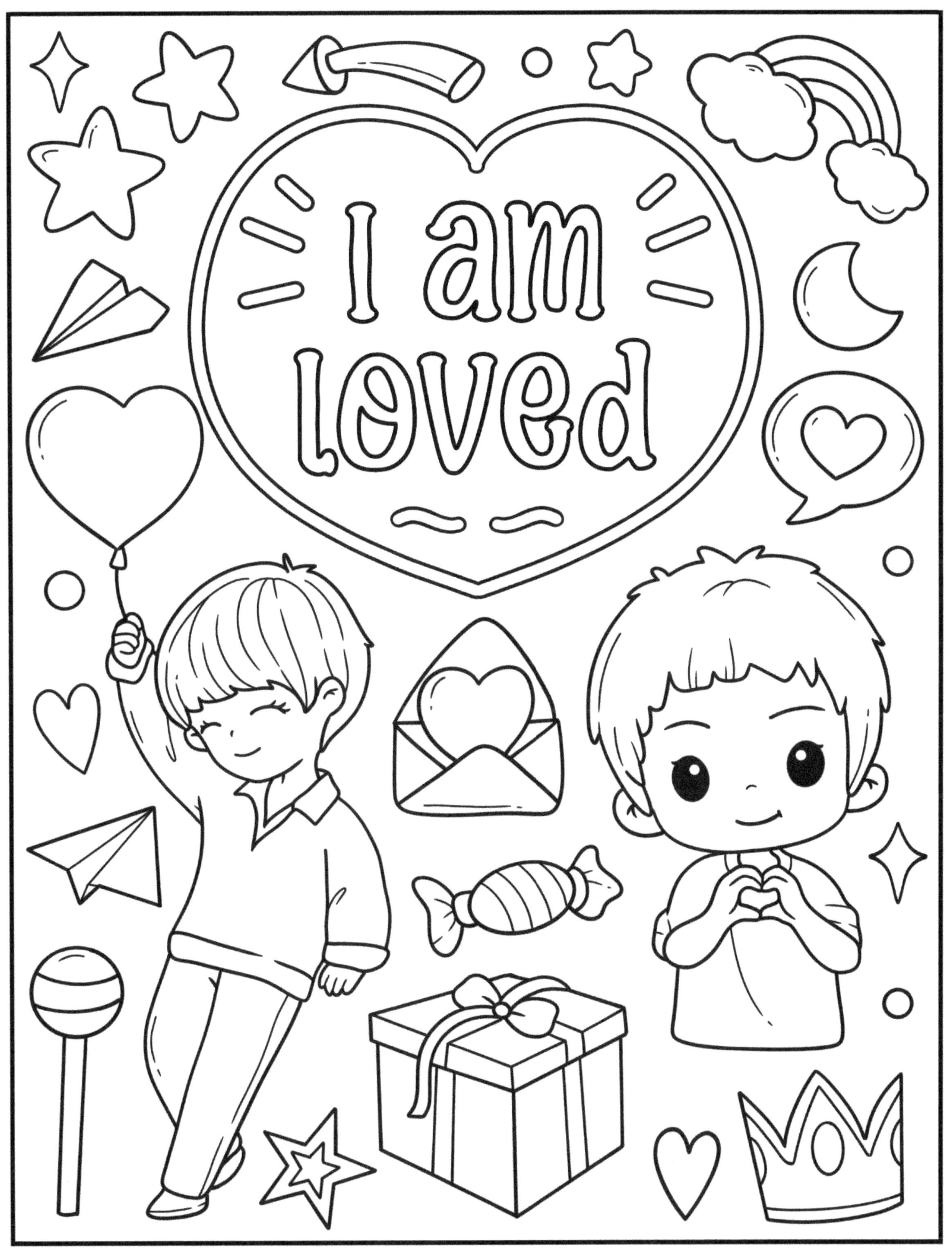
I am loved

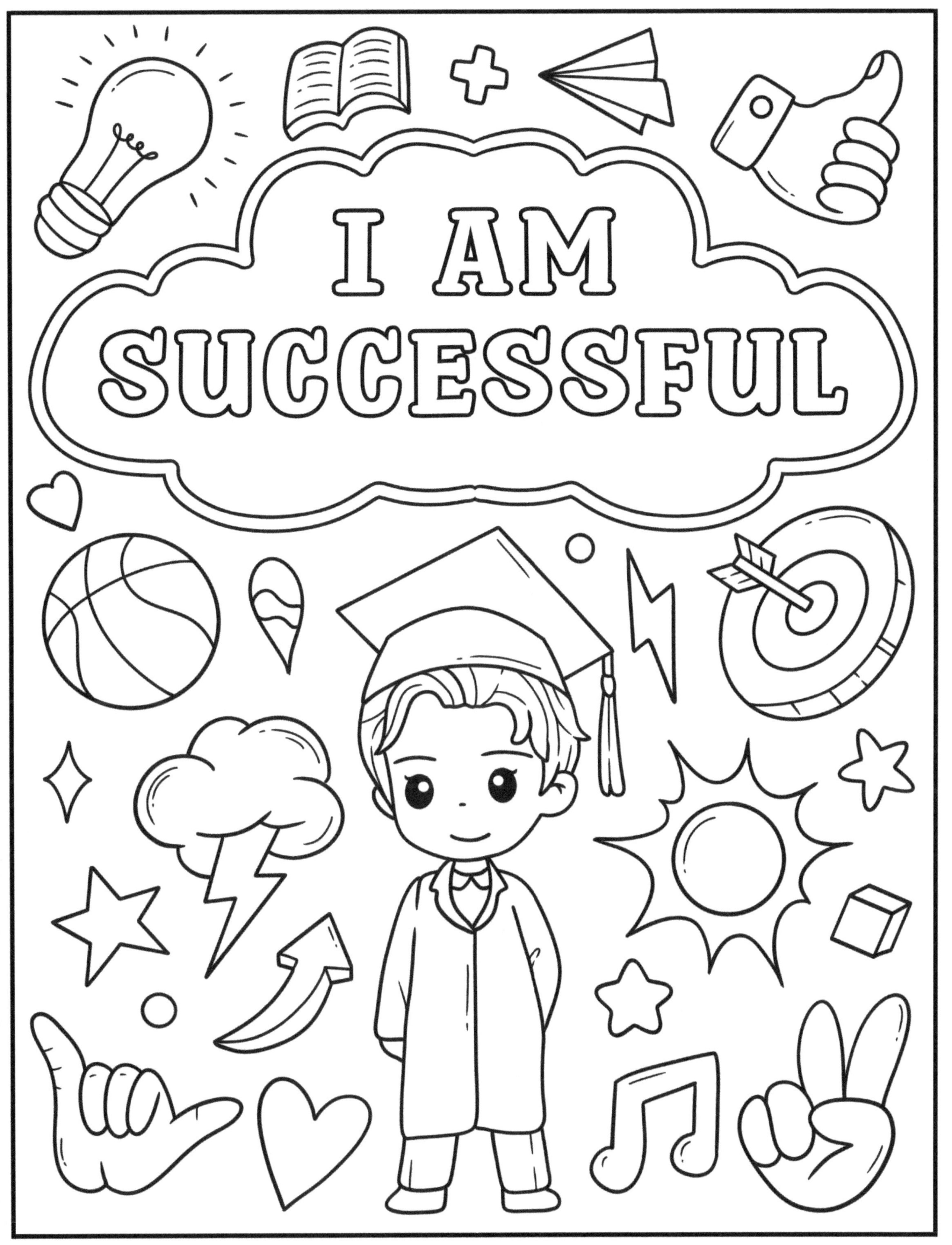
I AM
SUCCESSFUL

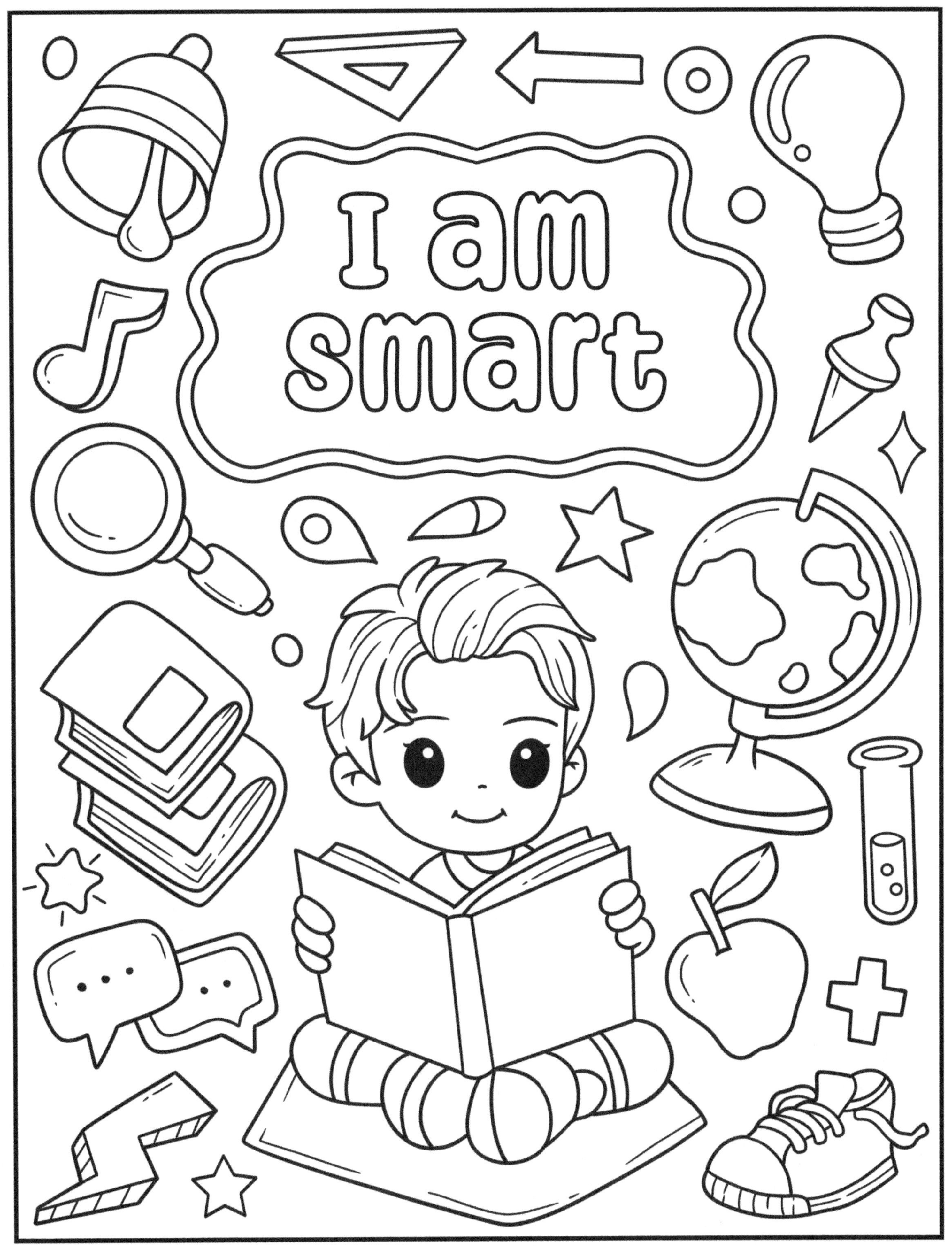
I am smart

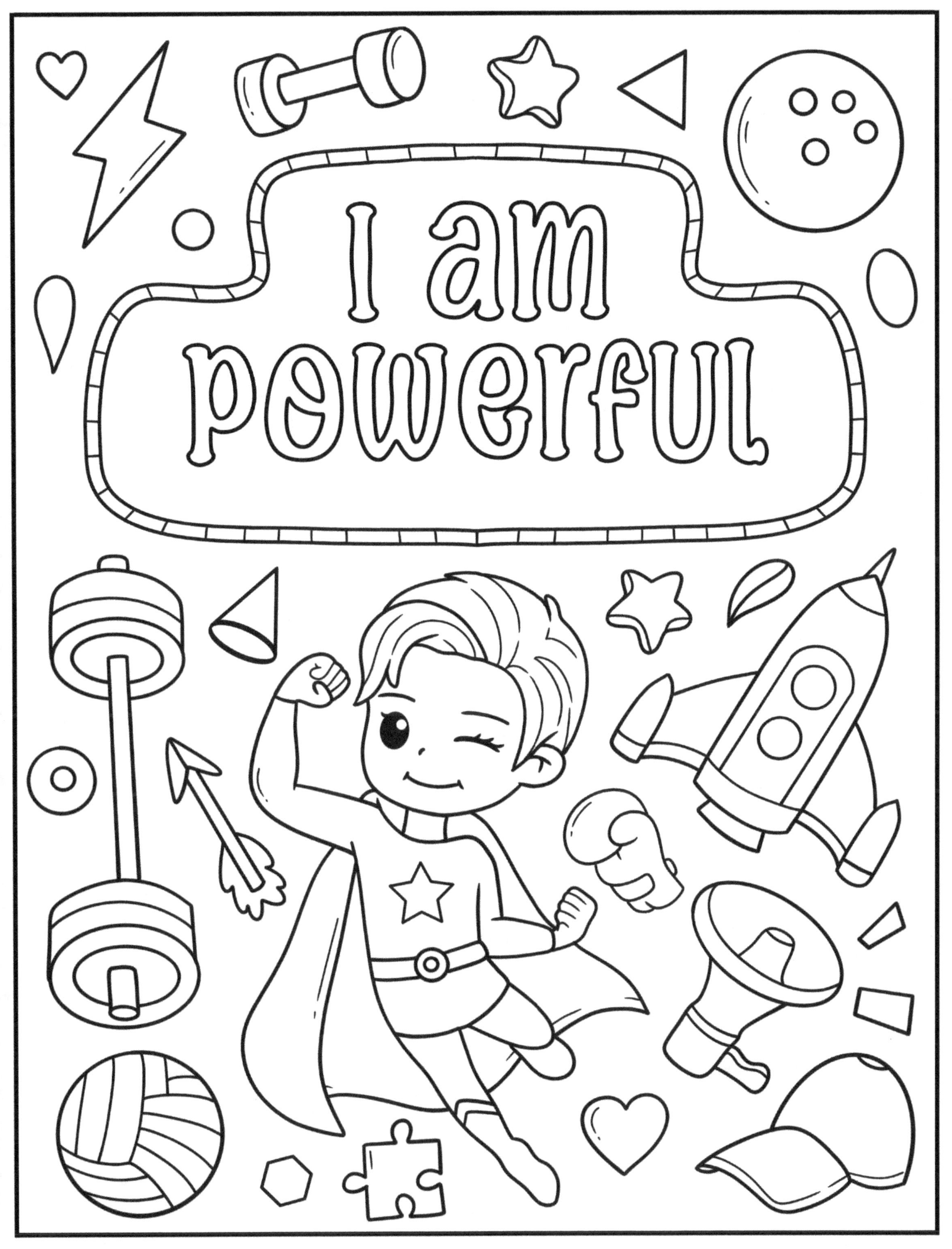
I am
powerful

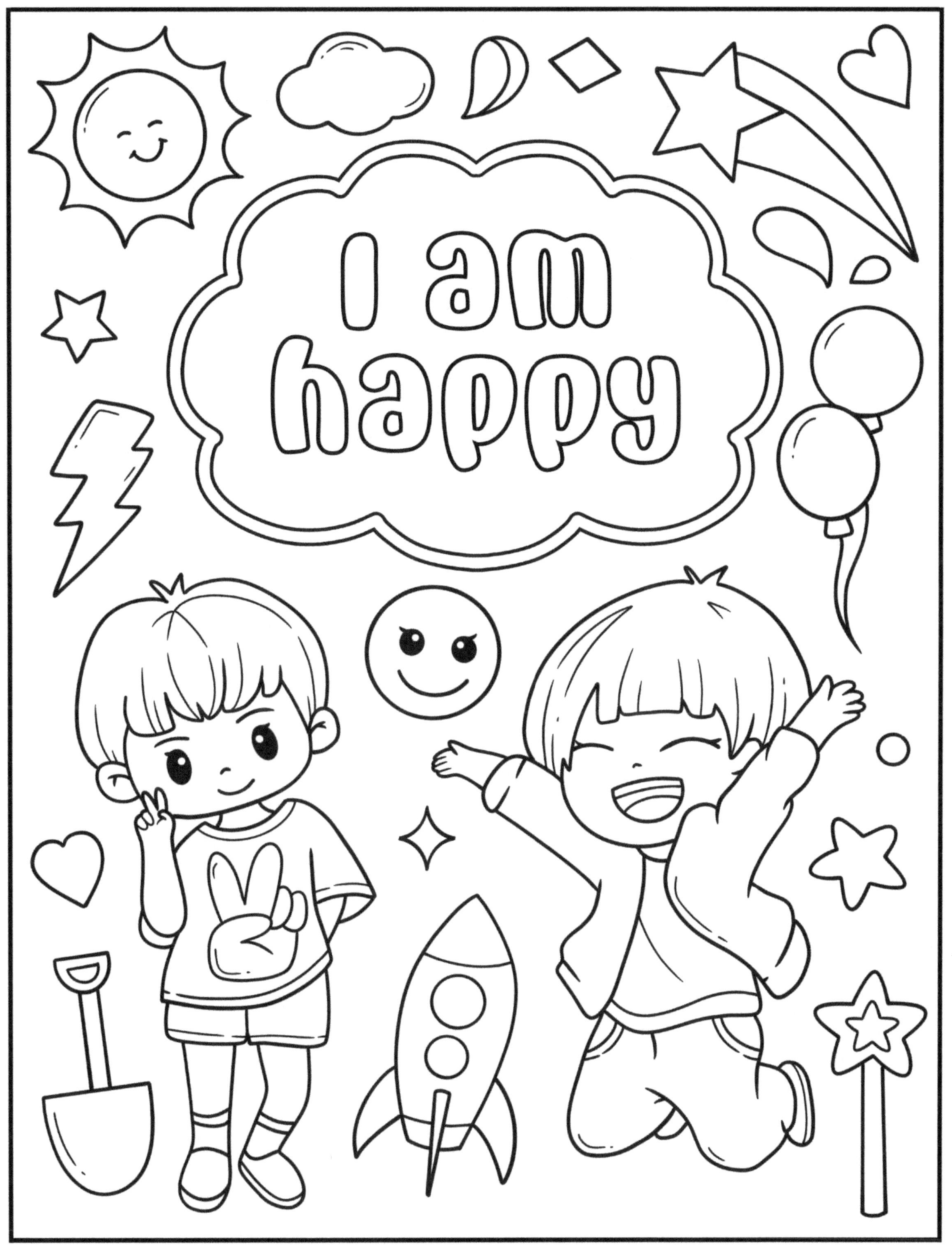
I am
happy

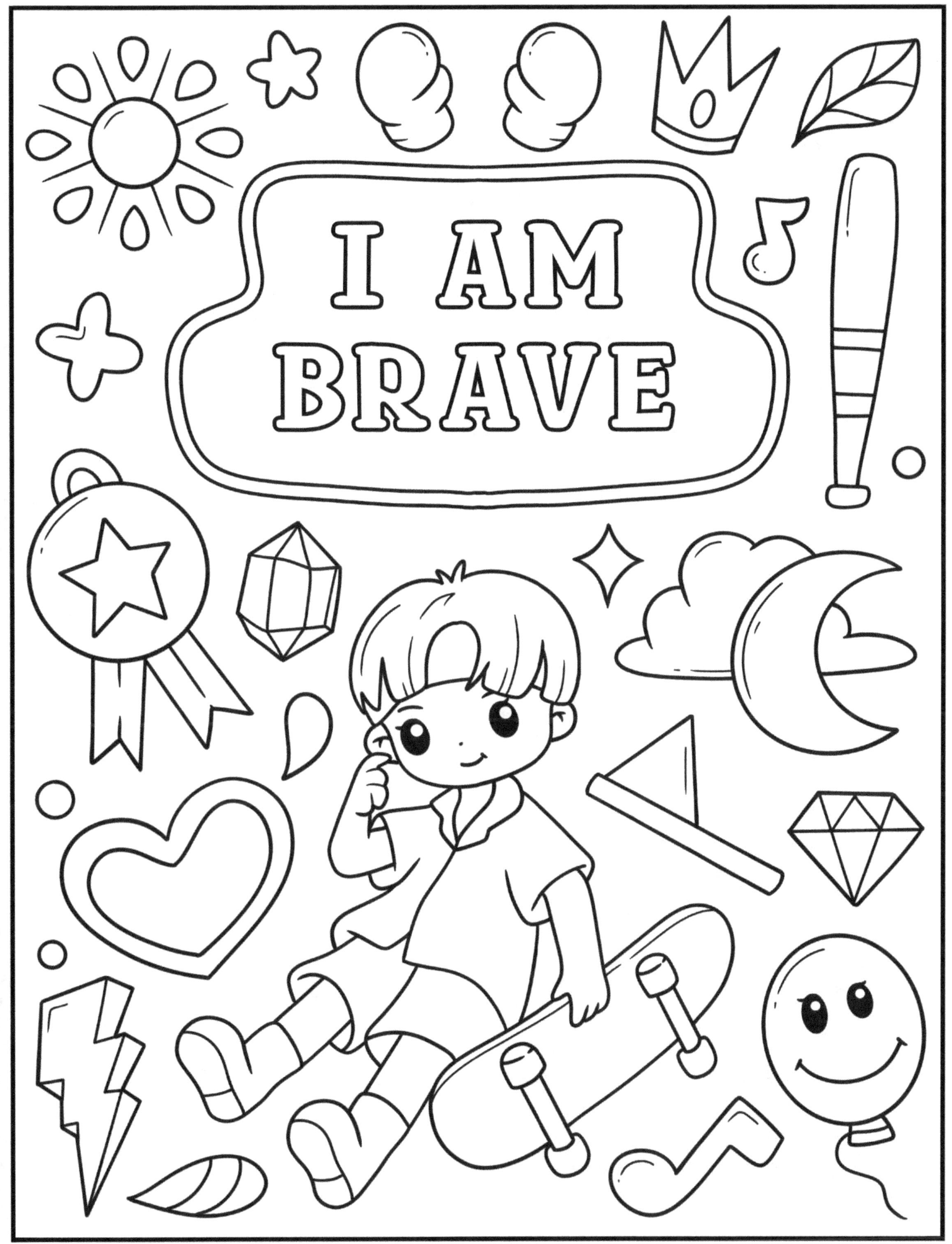
I AM
BRAVE

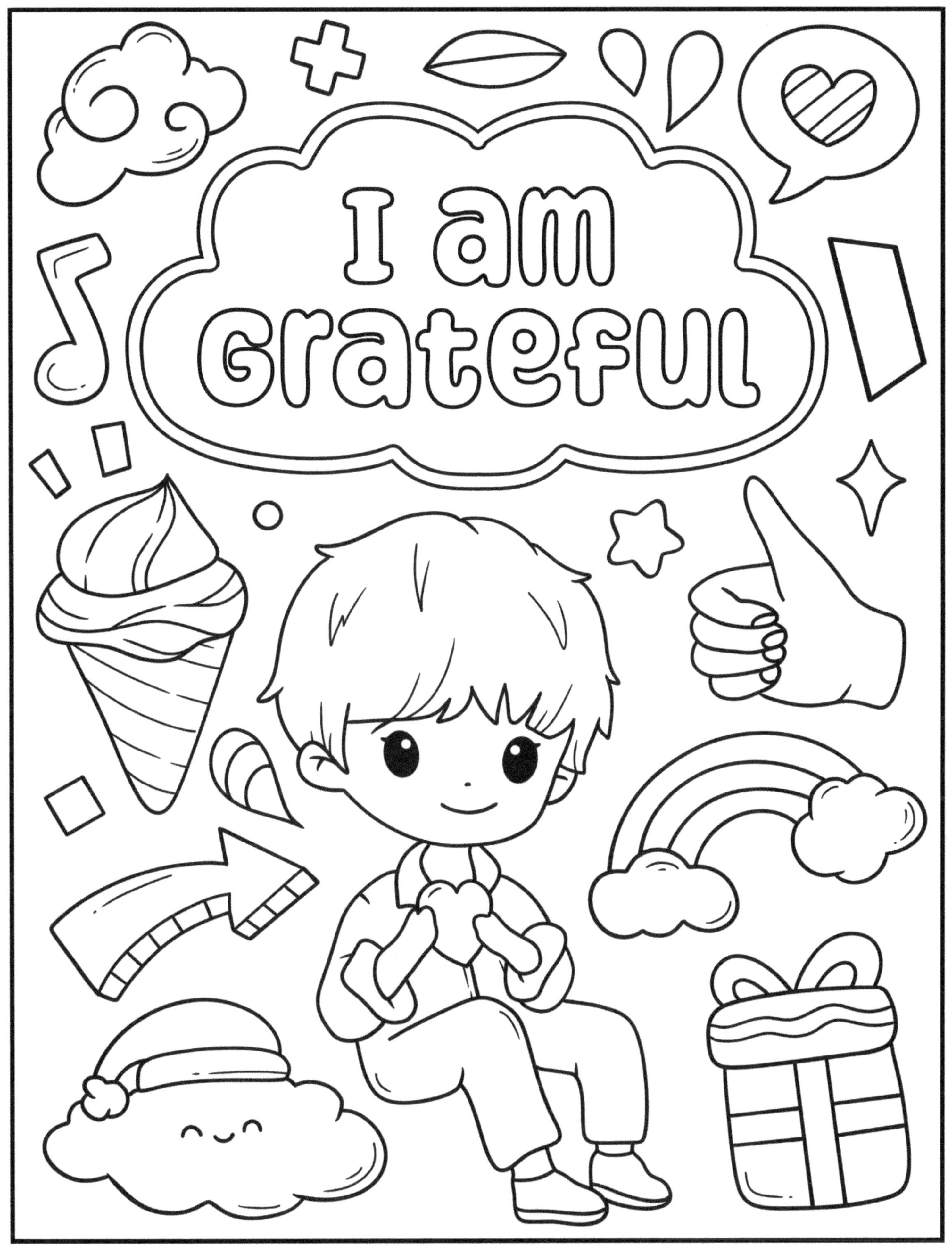
I am
grateful

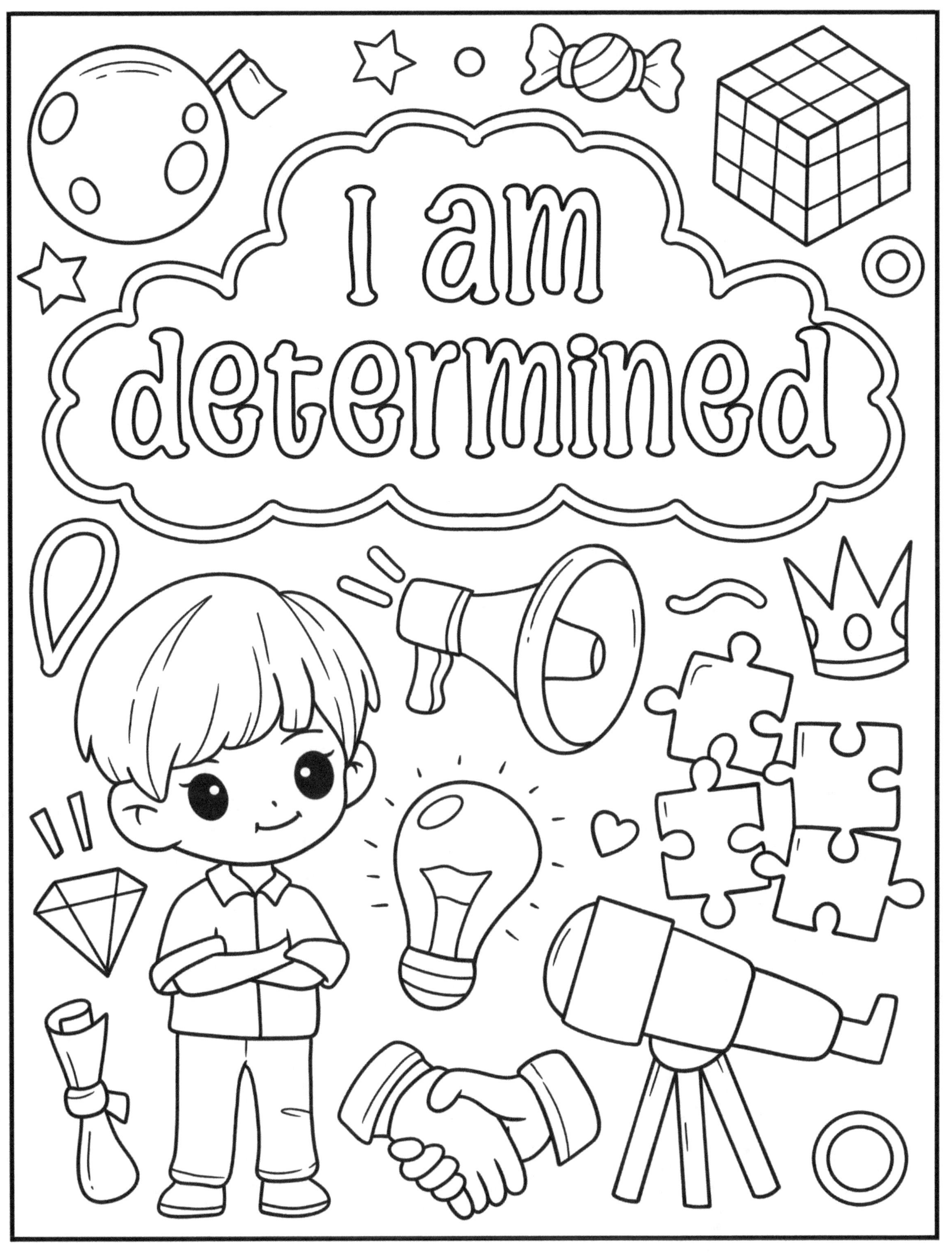
I am
determined

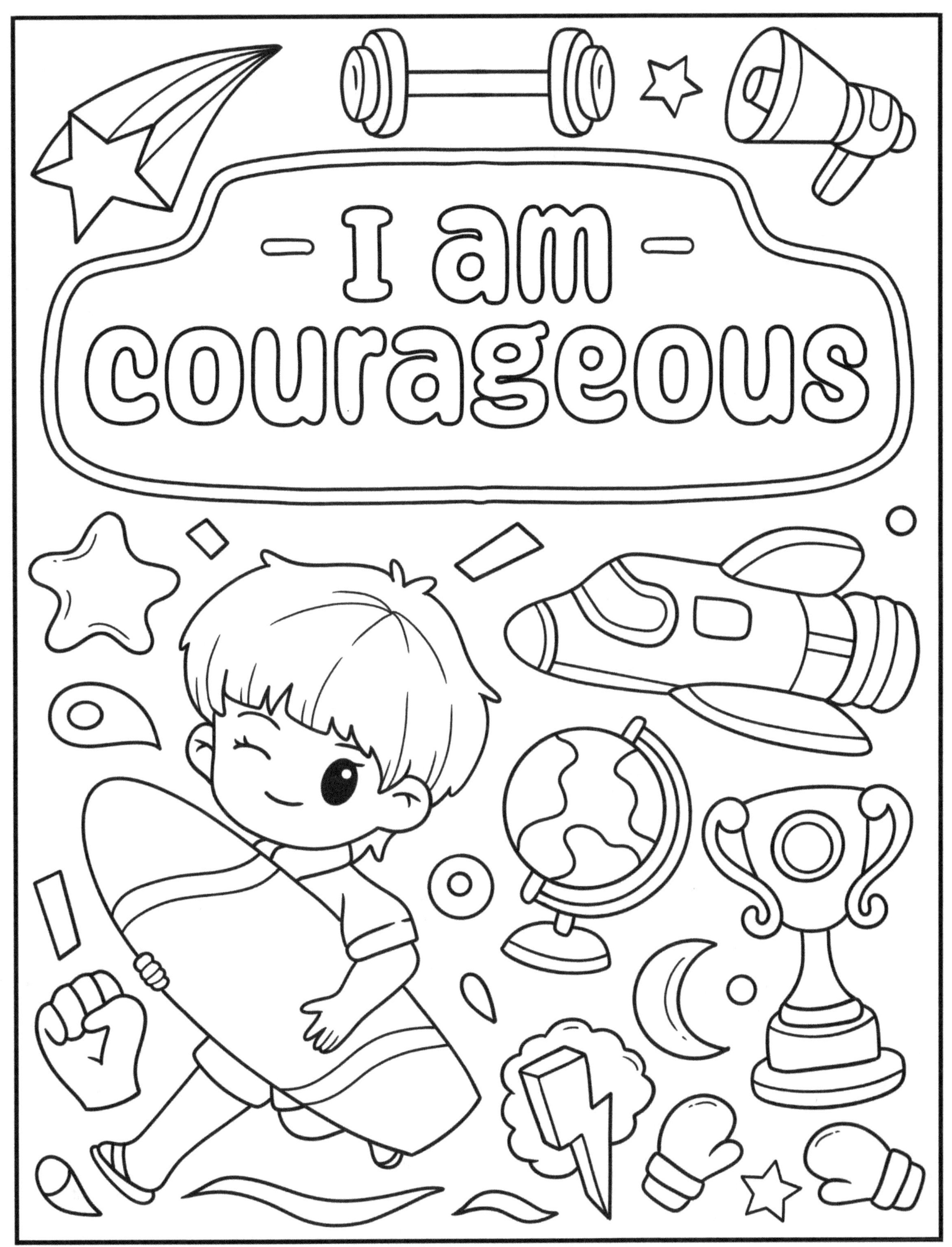
I am
courageous

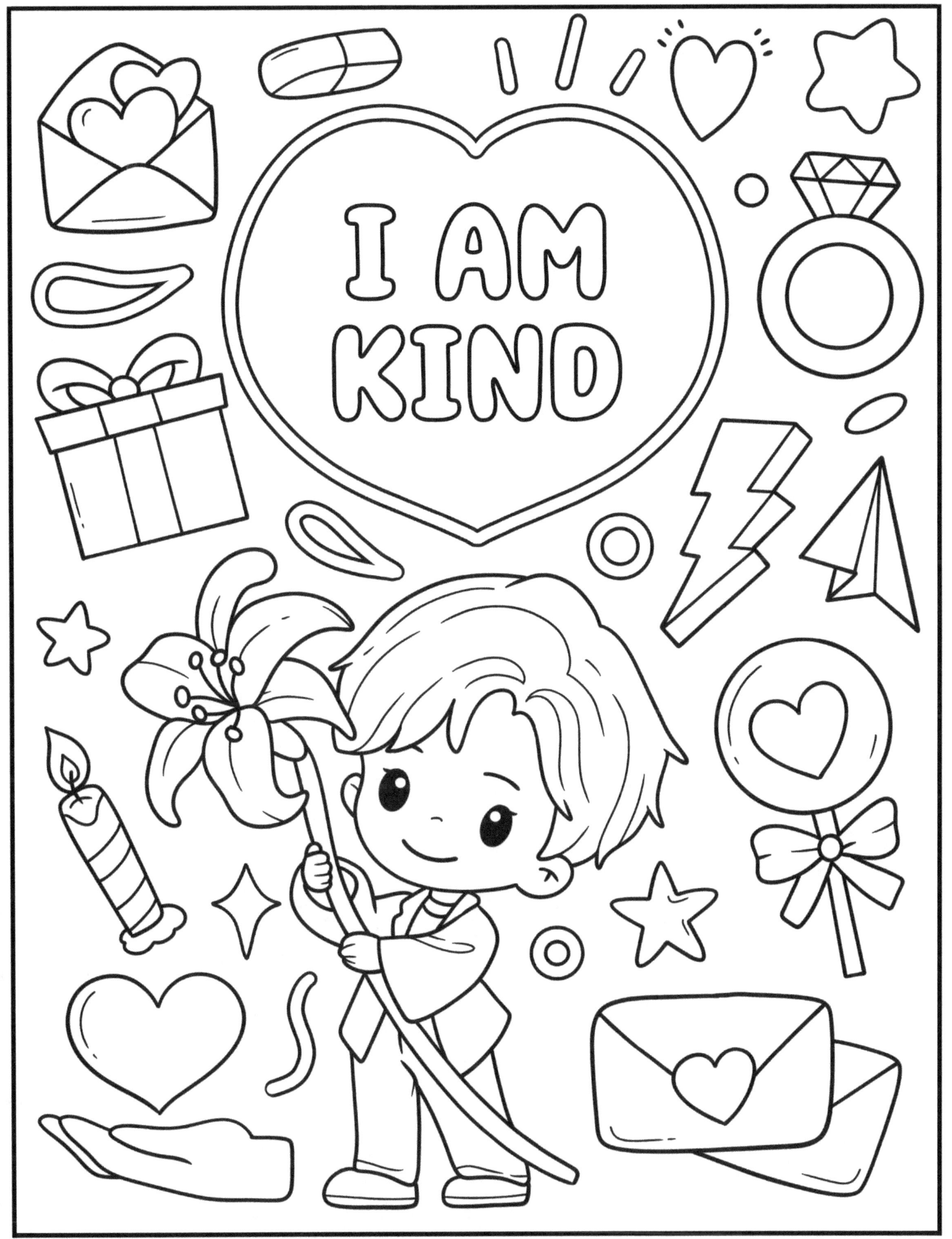
I AM
KIND

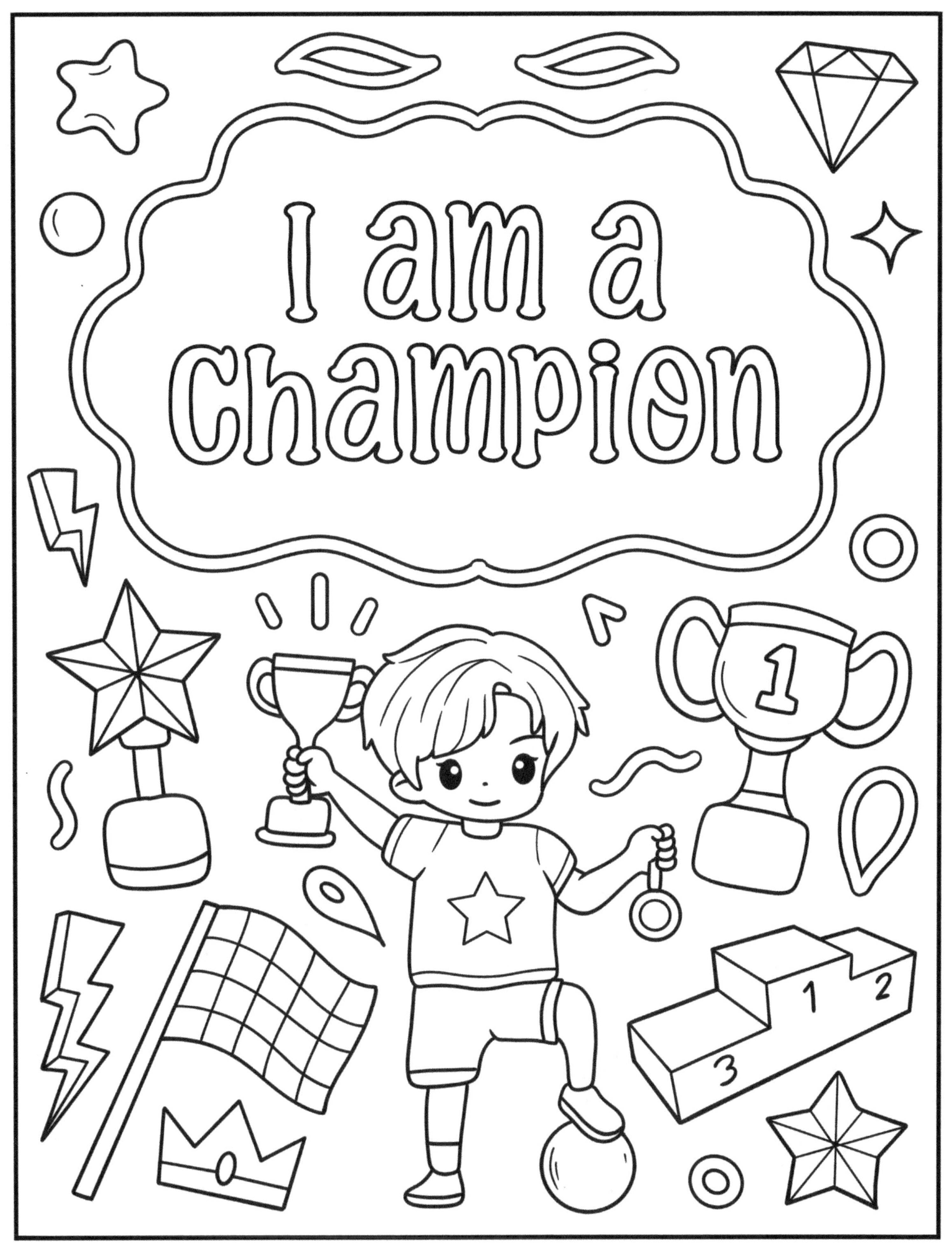
I am a Champion
1
1
2
3

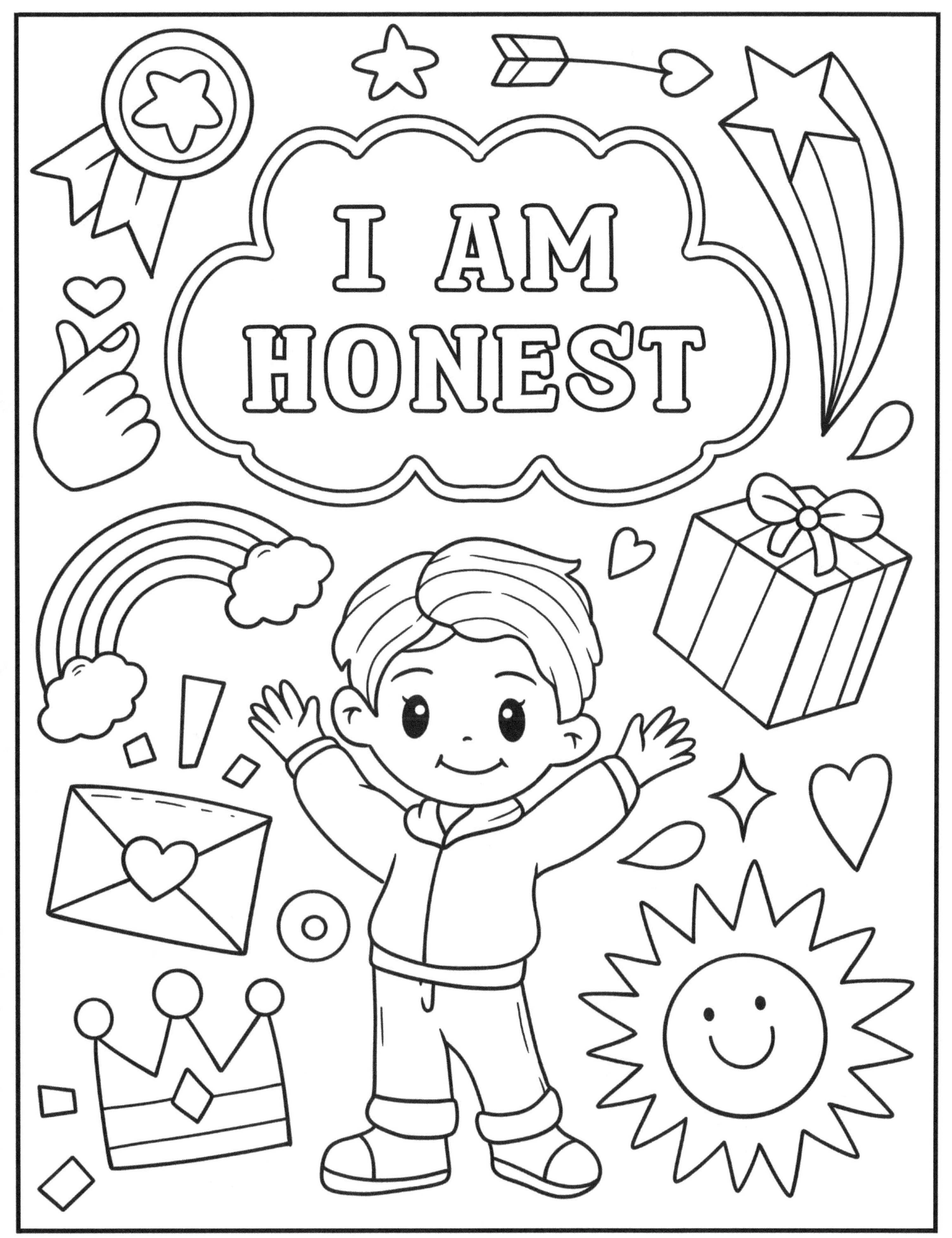
I AM
HONEST

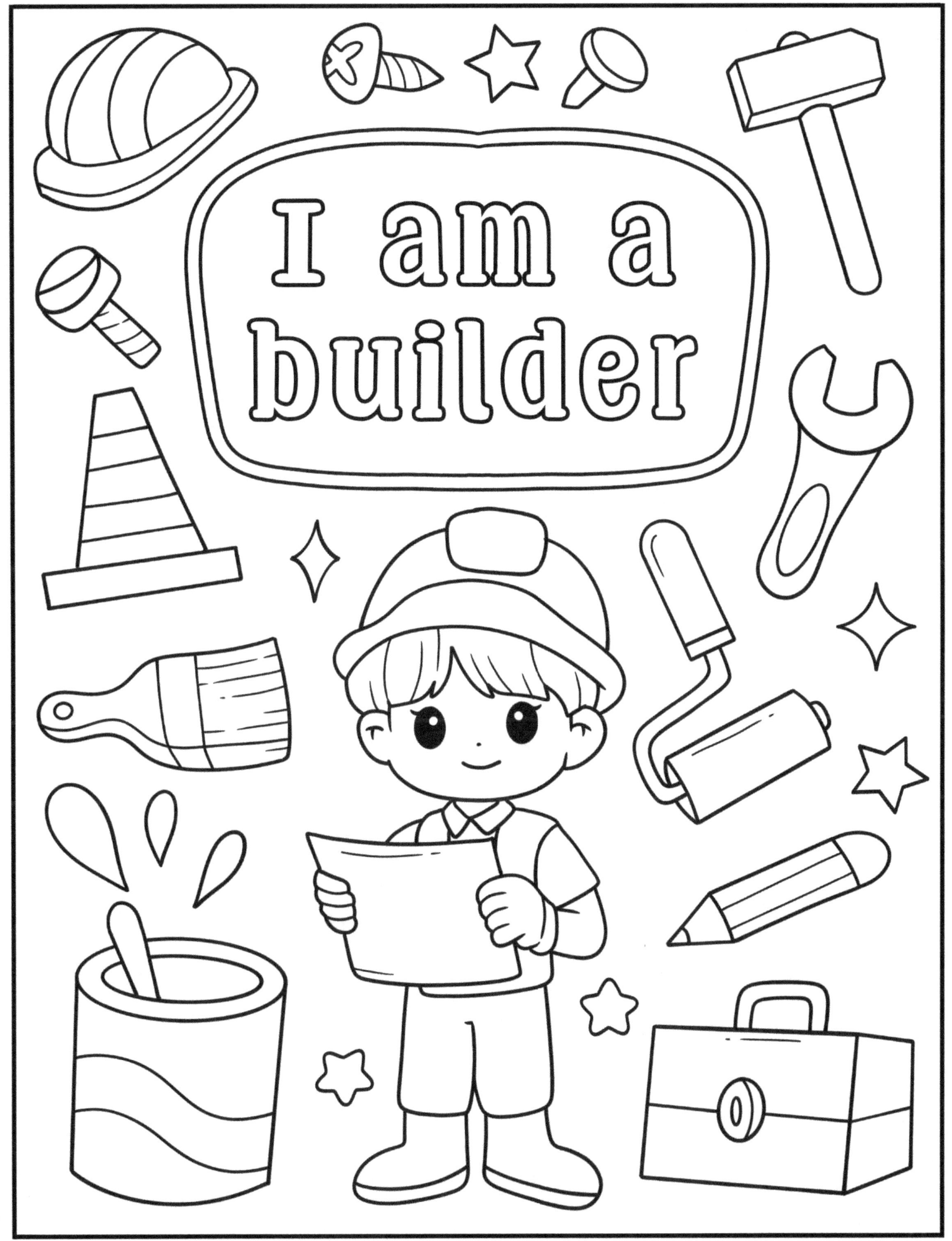
I am a builder

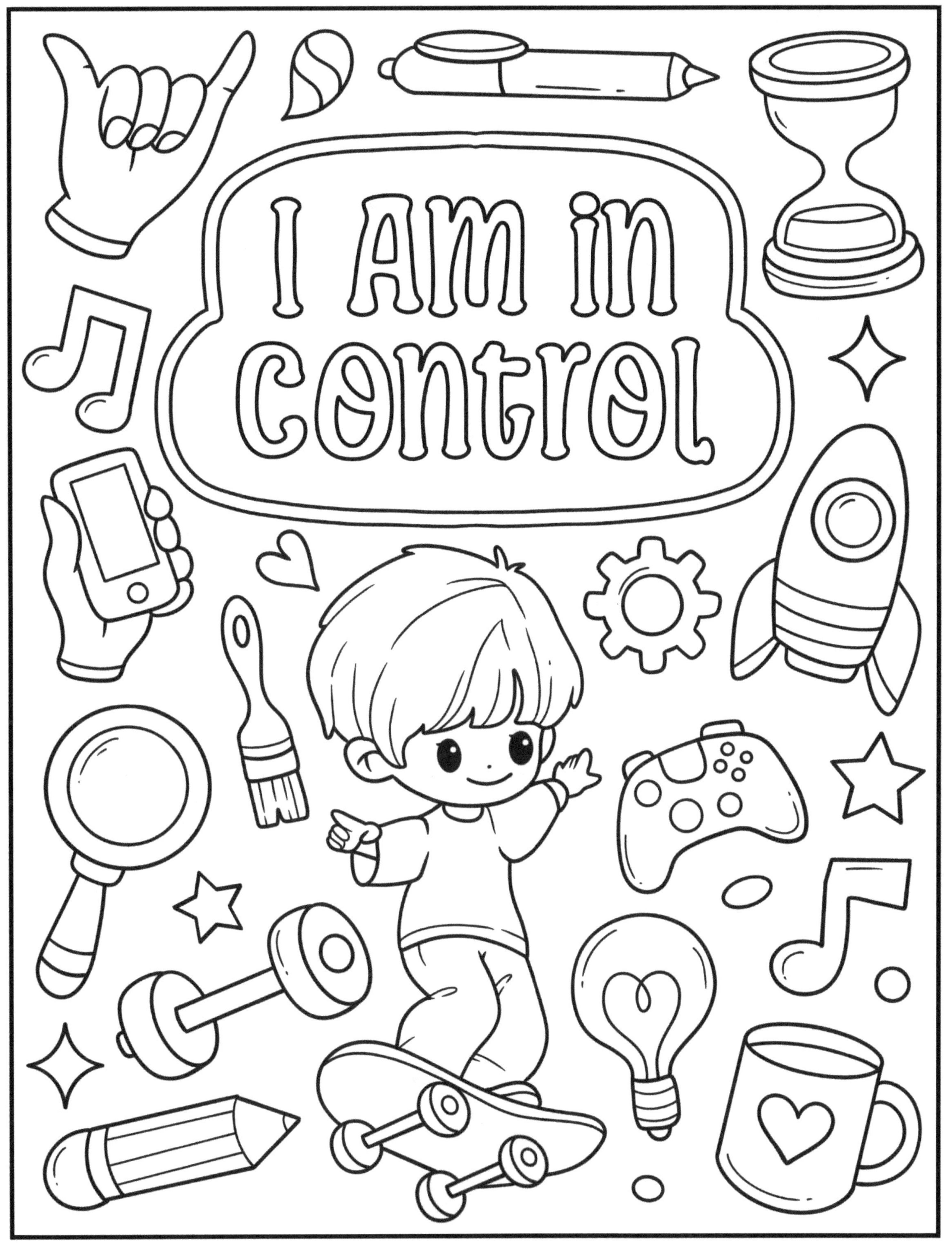
I Am in
Control

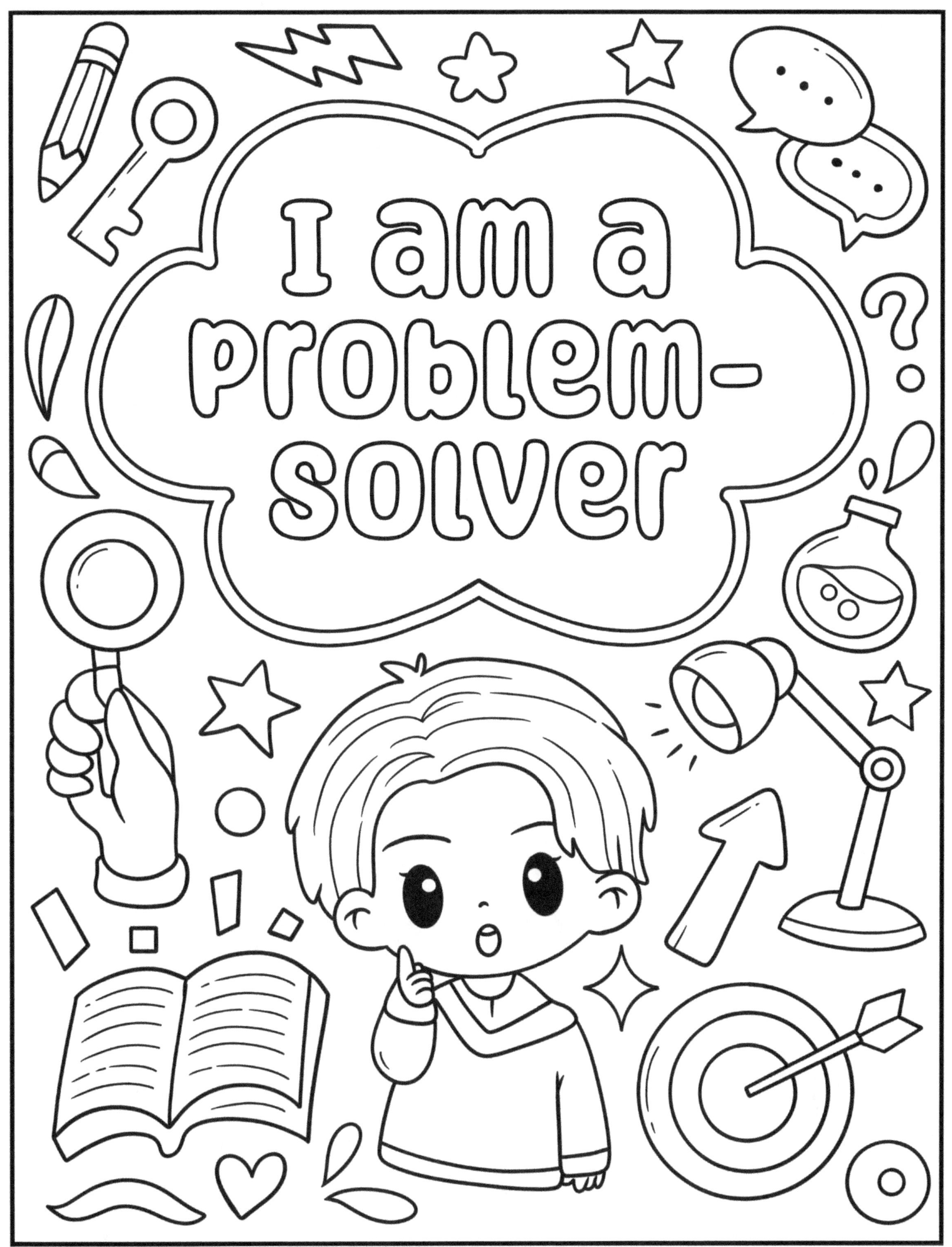
I am a problem-solver

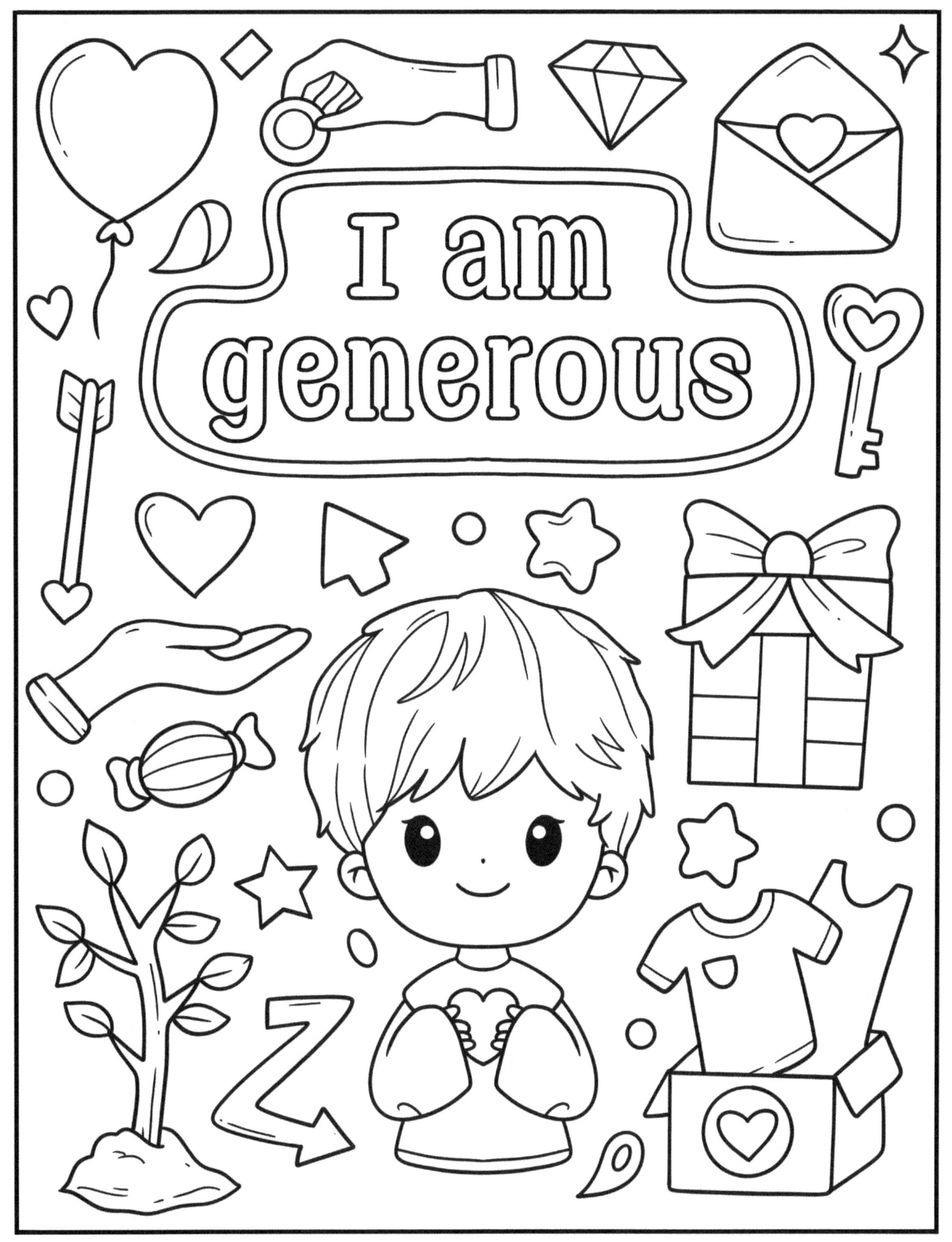
I am
generous

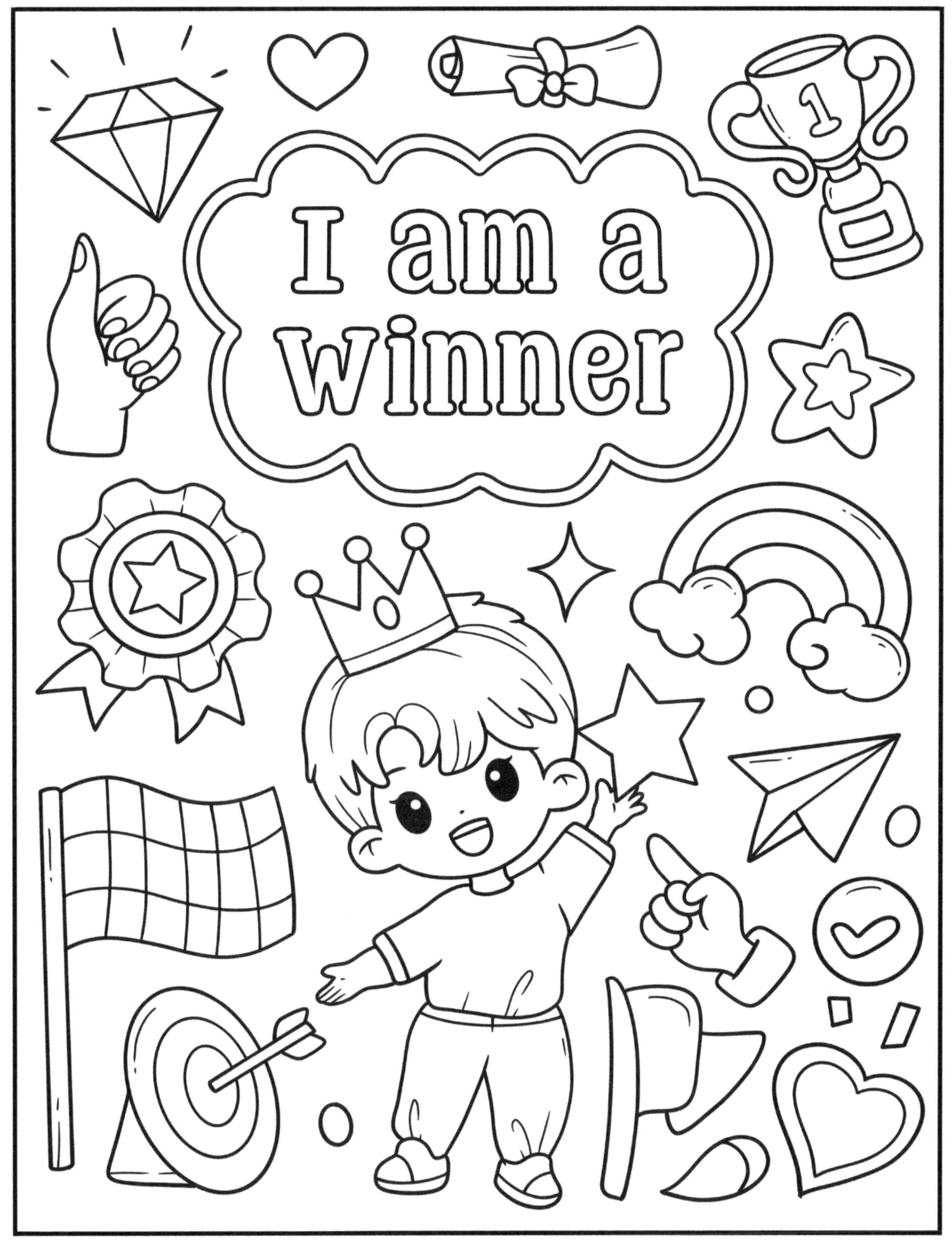
I am a
winner
1

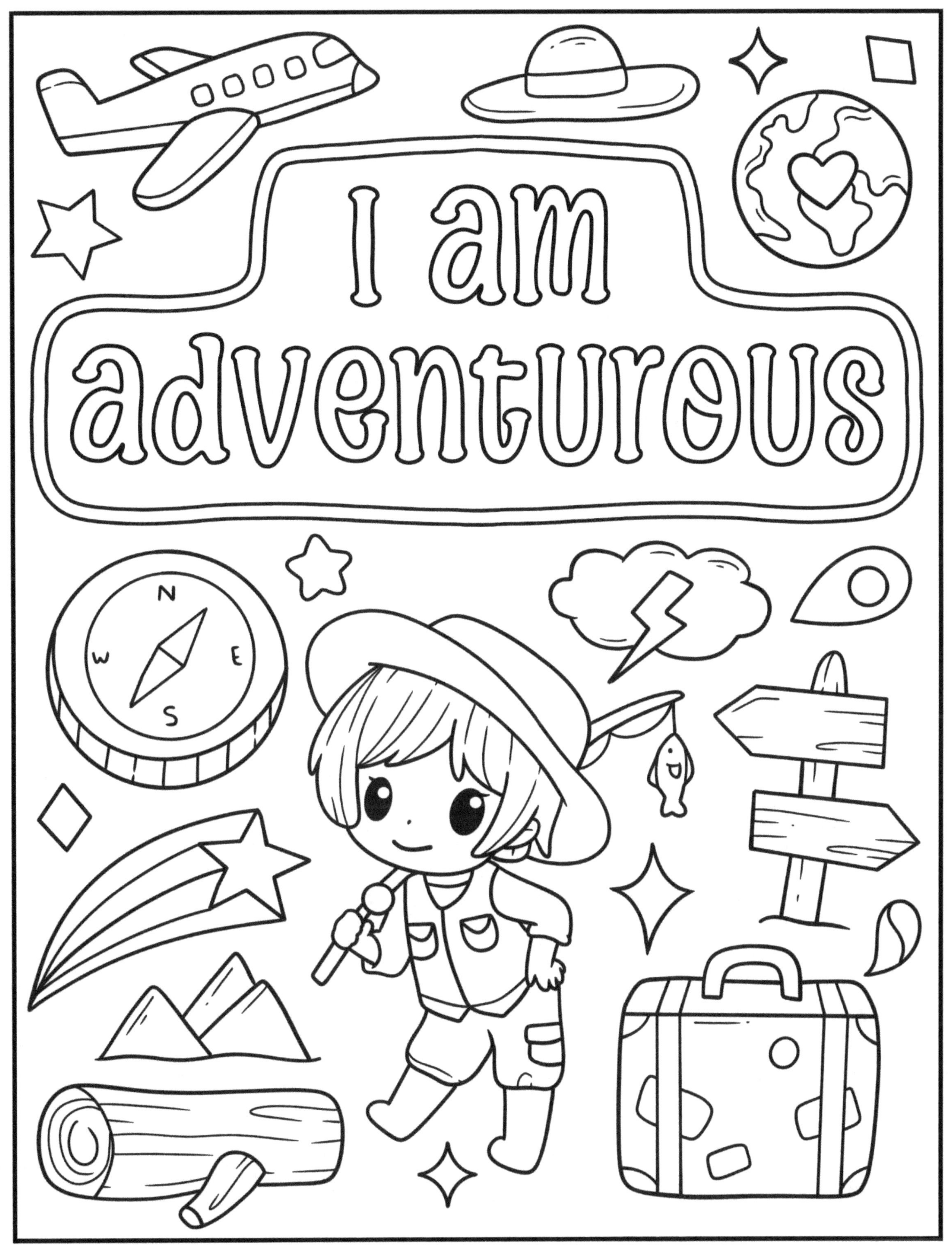
I am adventurous
N
W
E
S

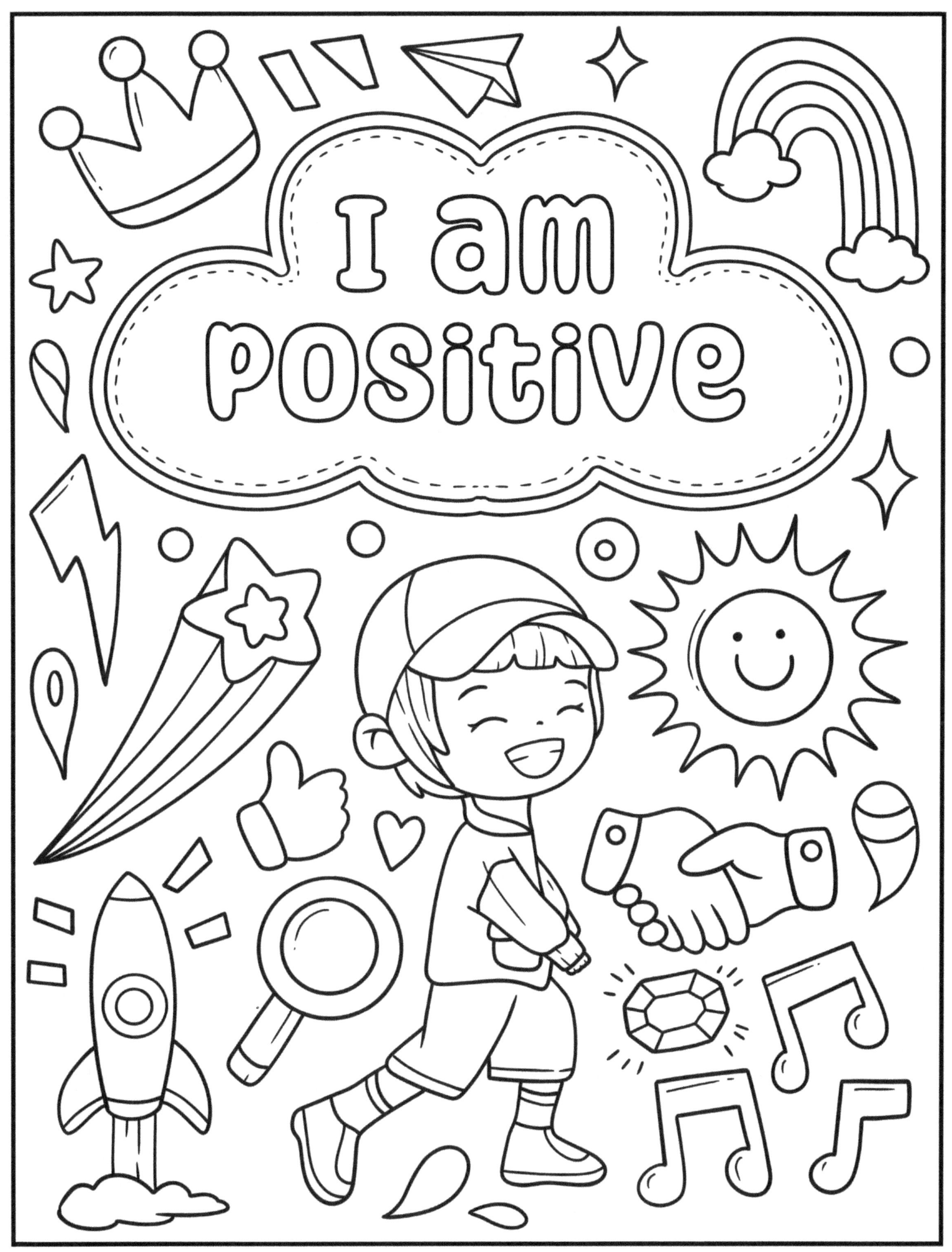
I am
positive

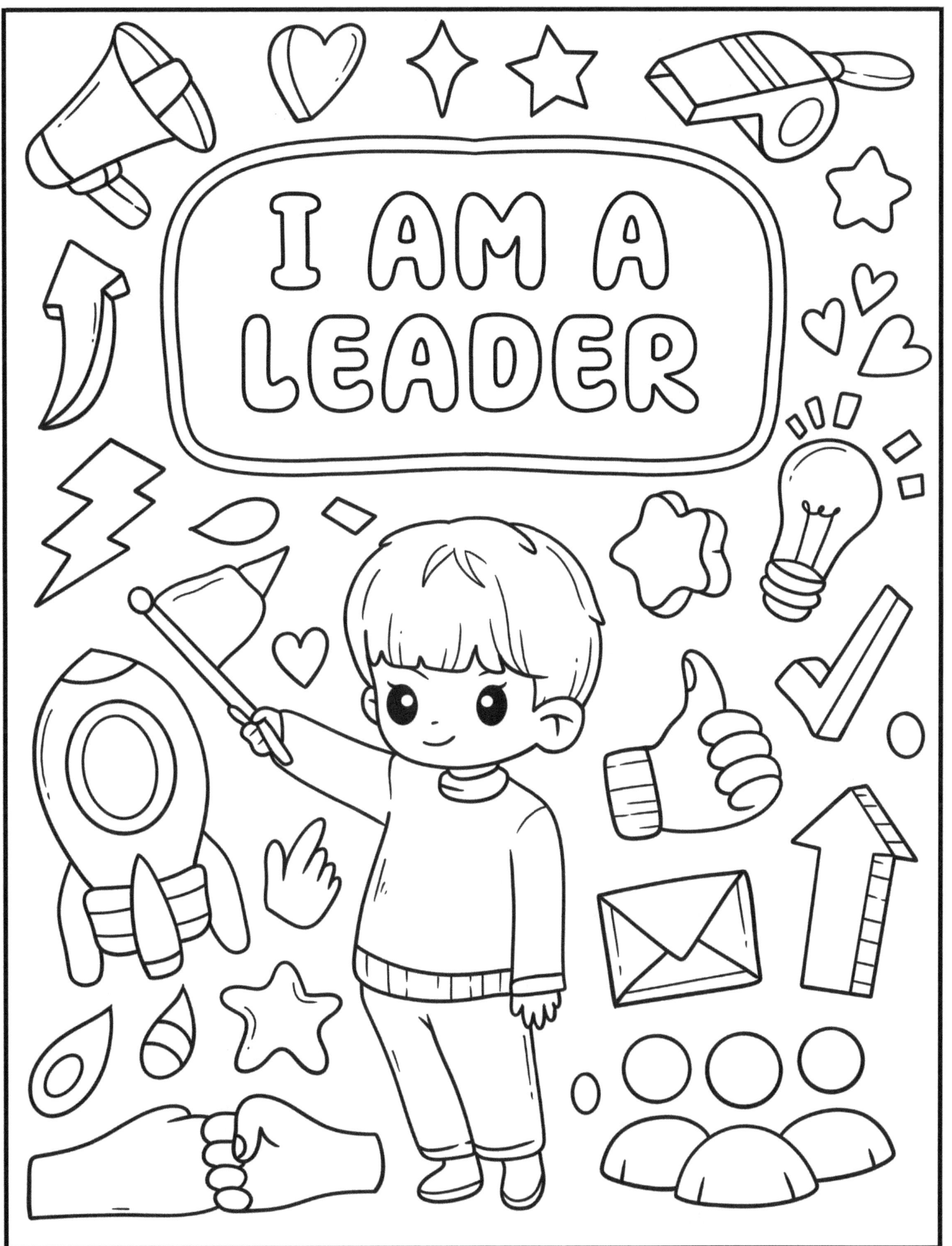
I AM A
LEADER

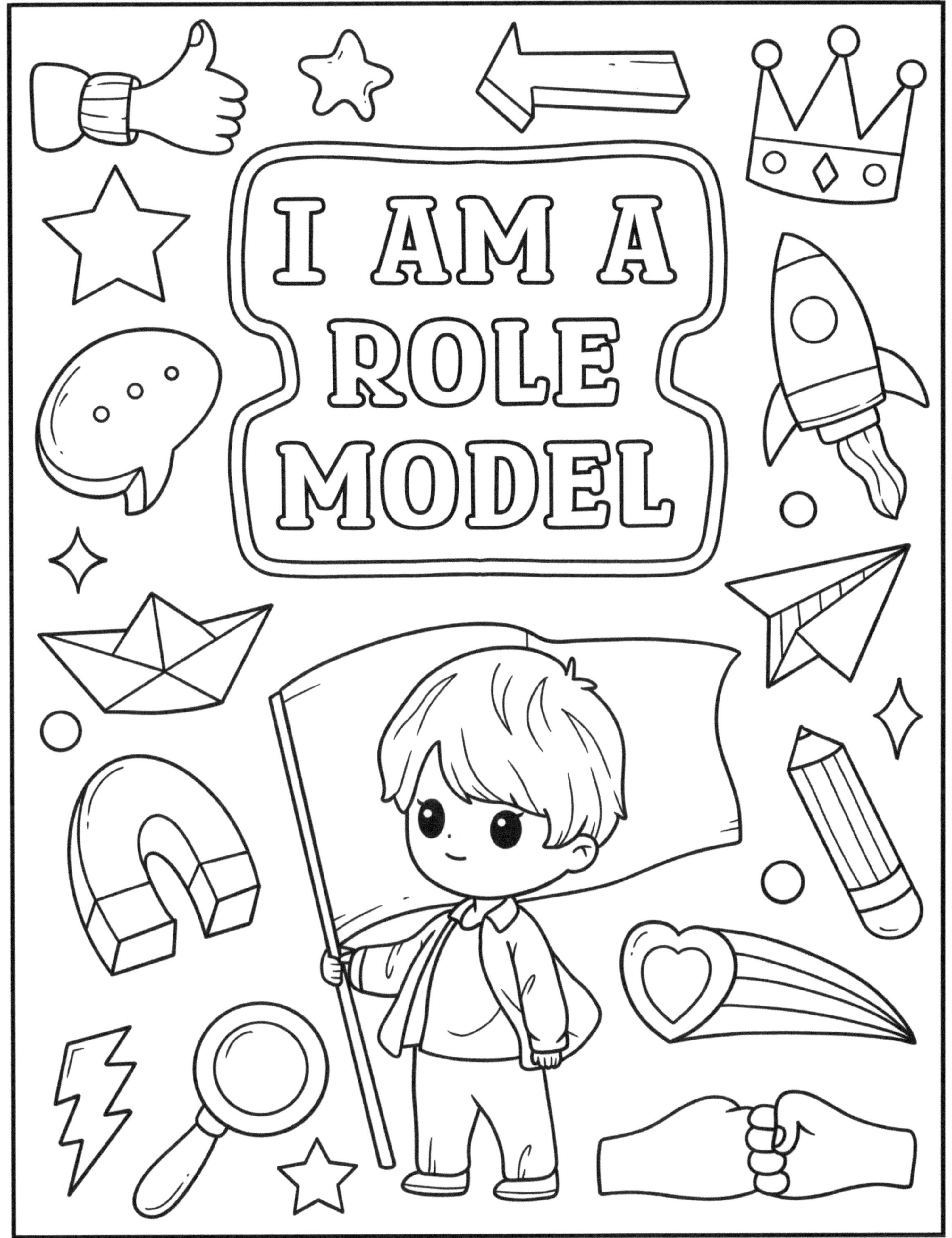
I AM A
ROLE
MODEL

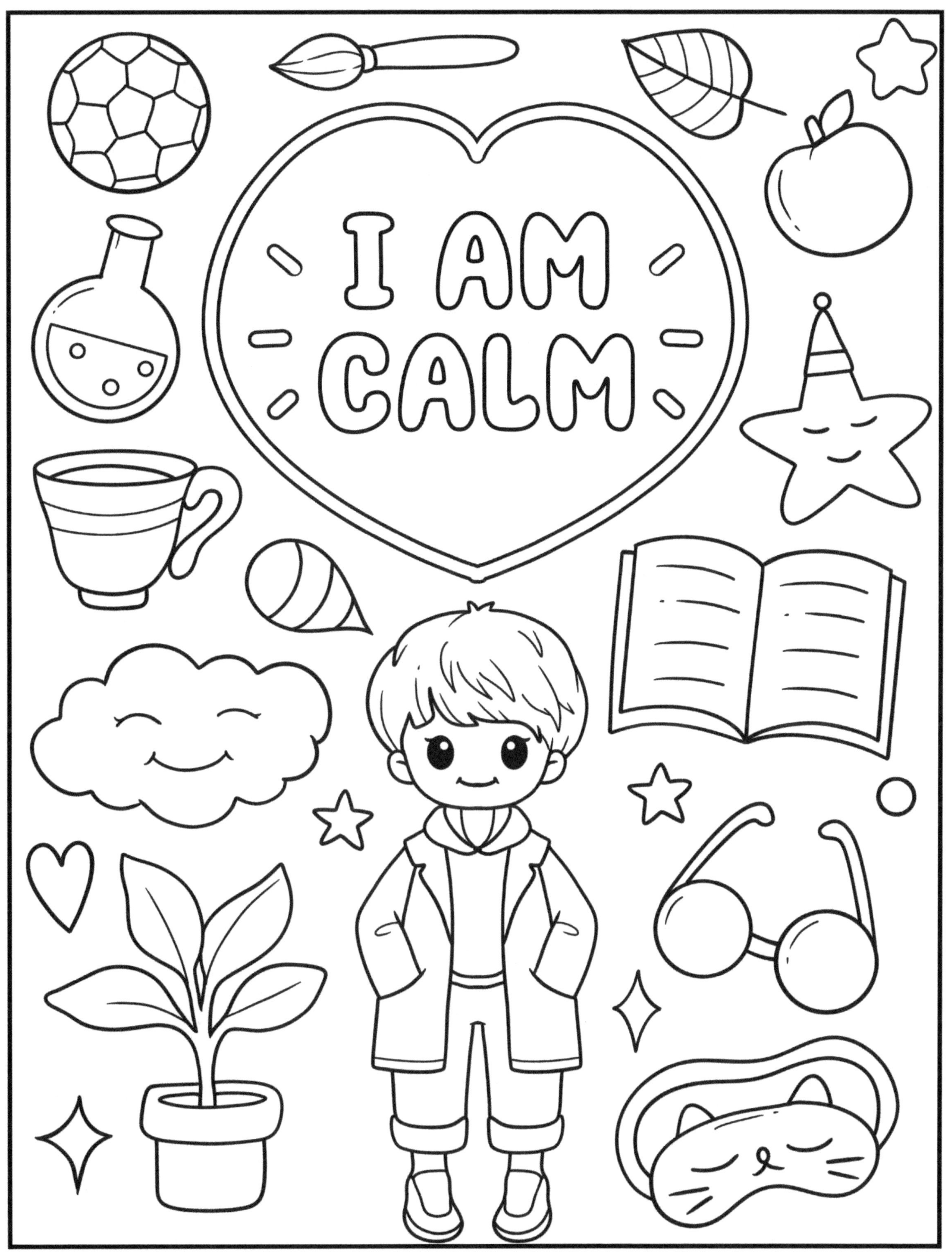
I AM
CALM

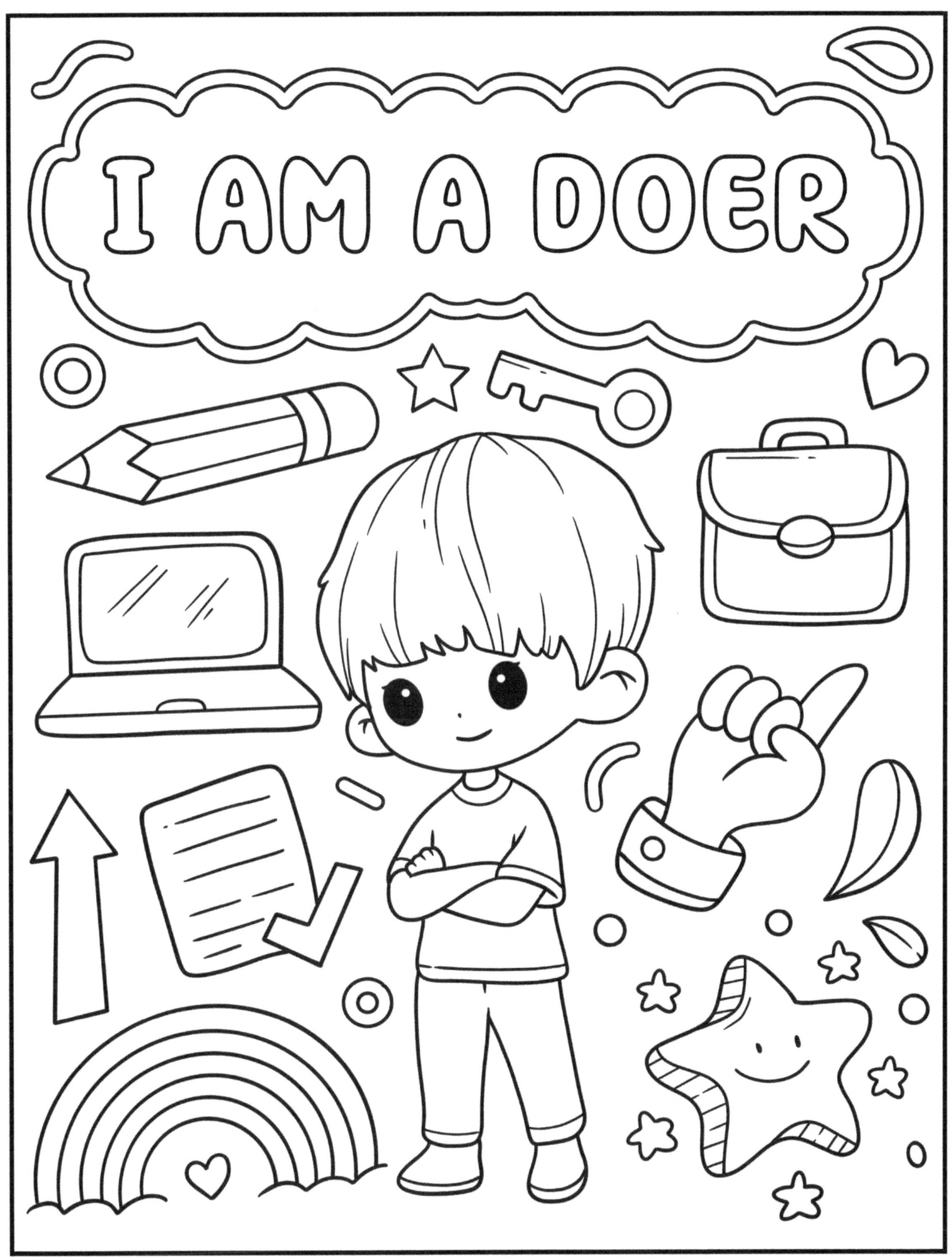
I AM A DOER

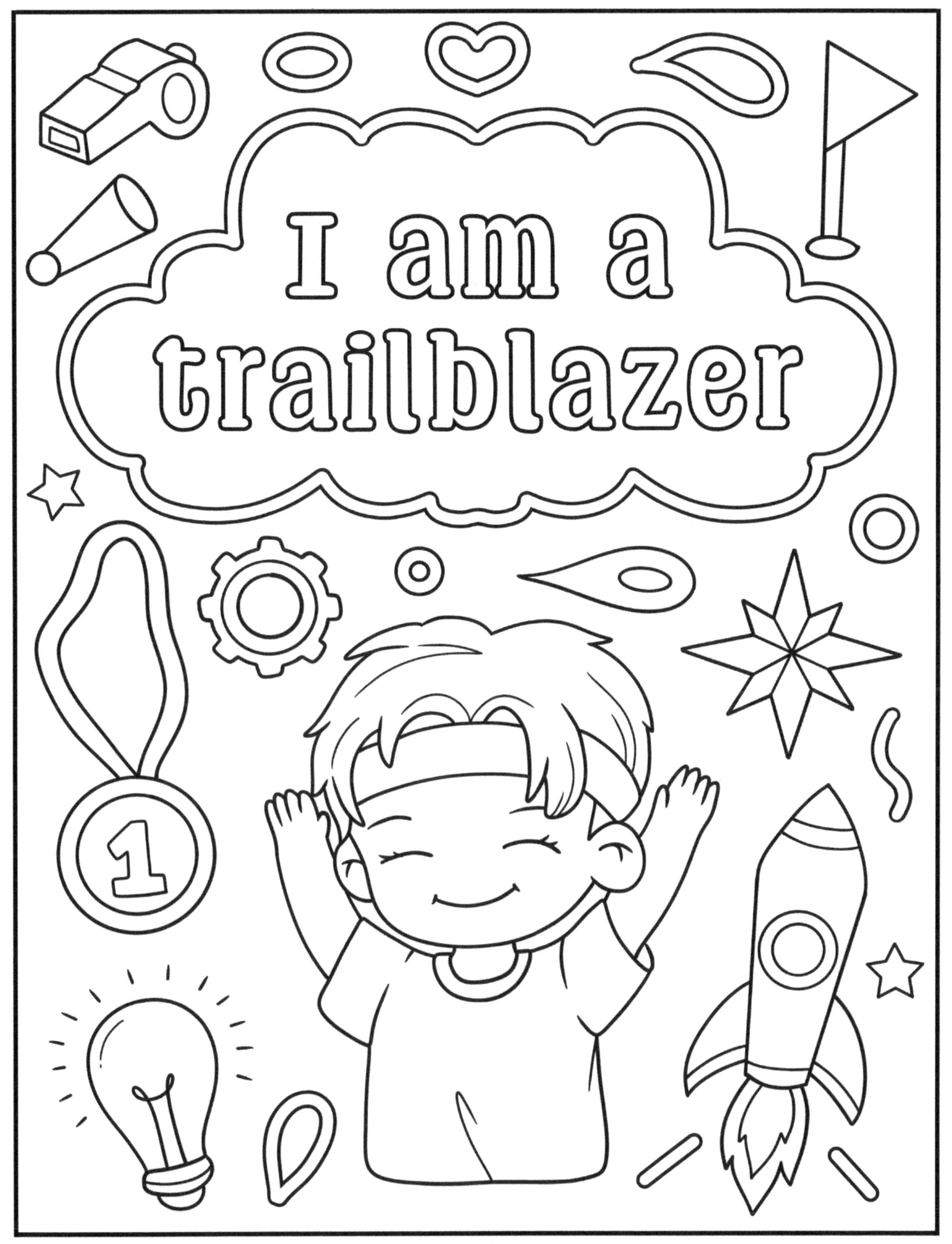
I am a trailblazer
1

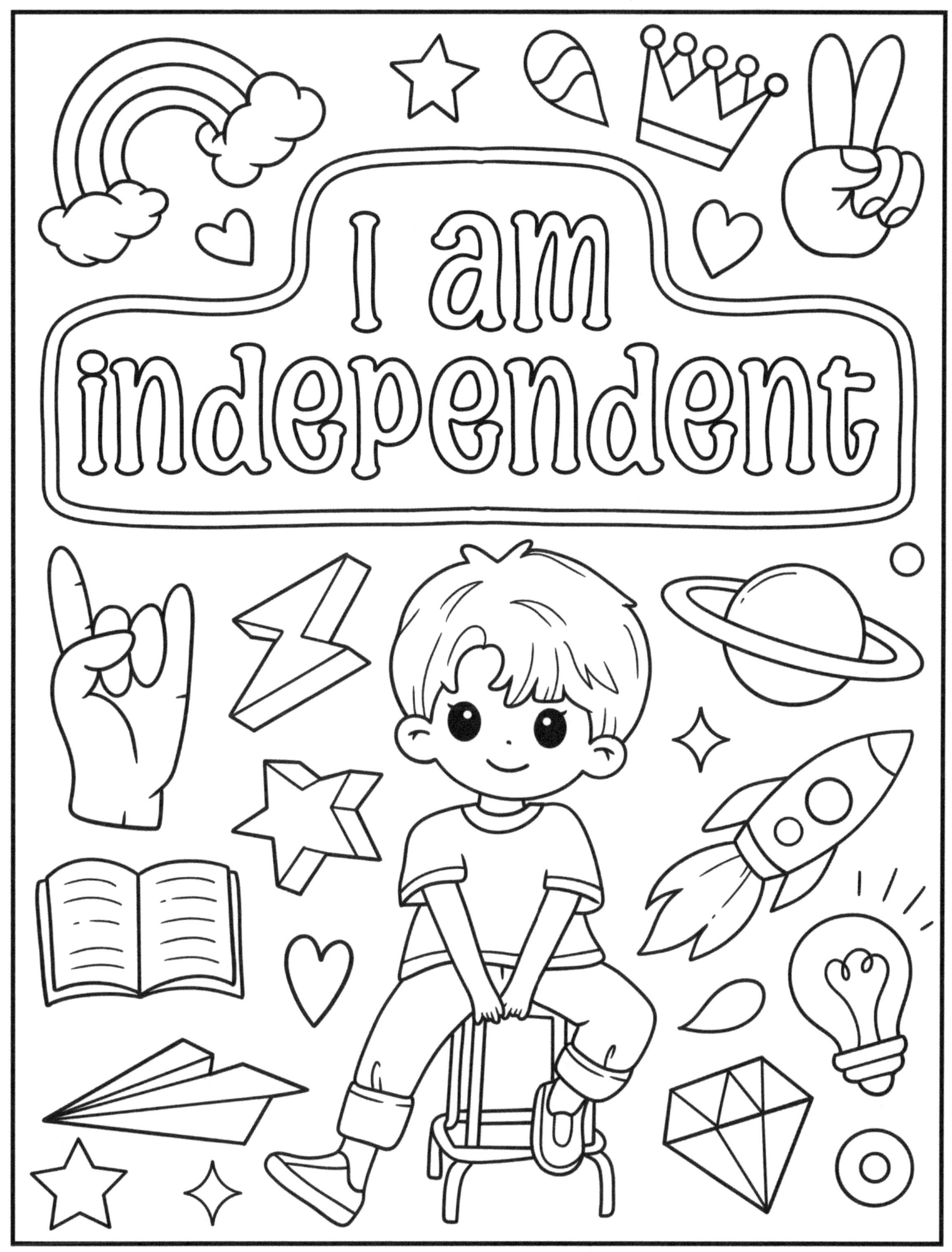
I am
independent

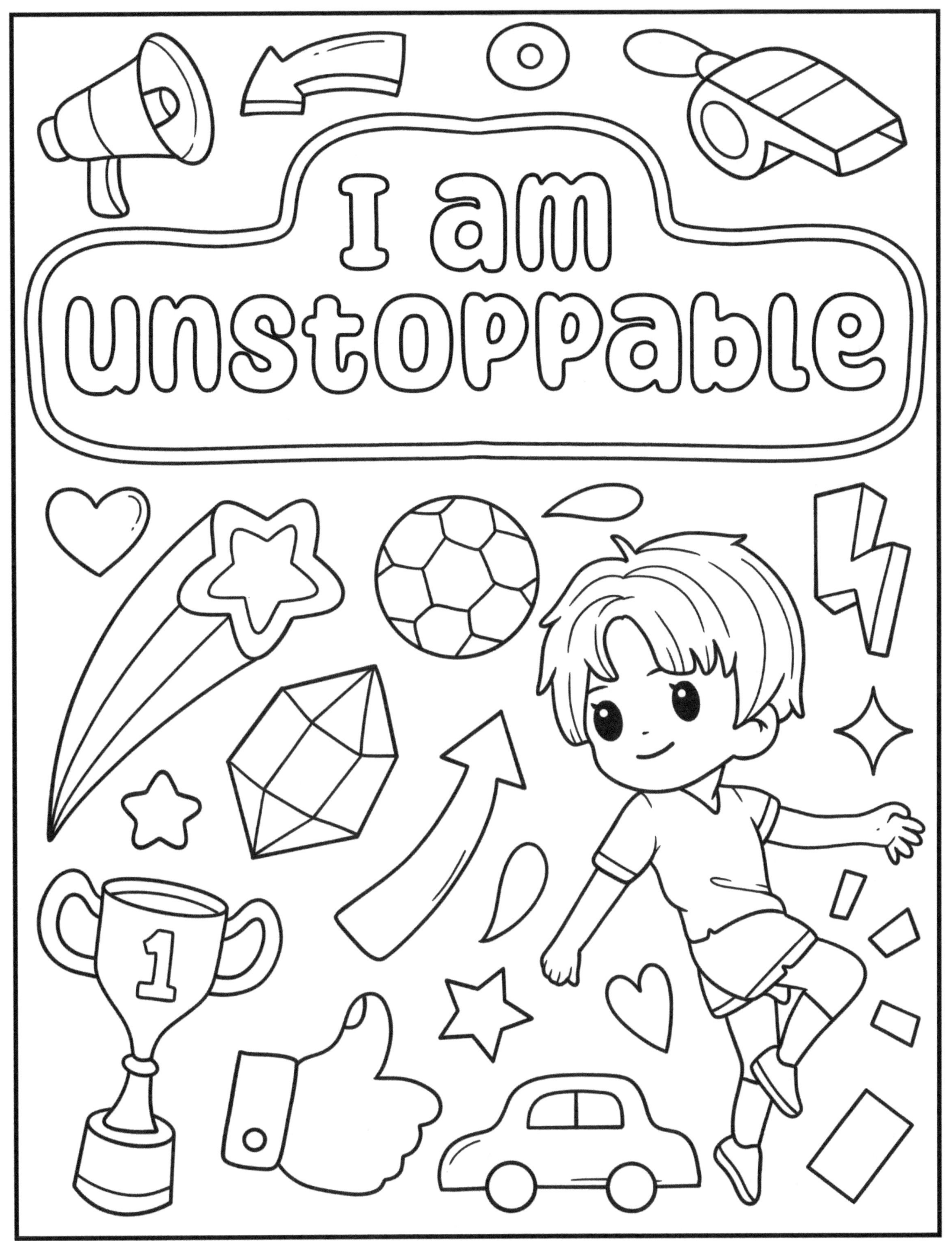
I am unstoppable
1

www.ingramcontent.com/pod-product-compliance
Lightning Source LLC
LaVergne TN
LVHW061255100826
845148LV00008B/1131